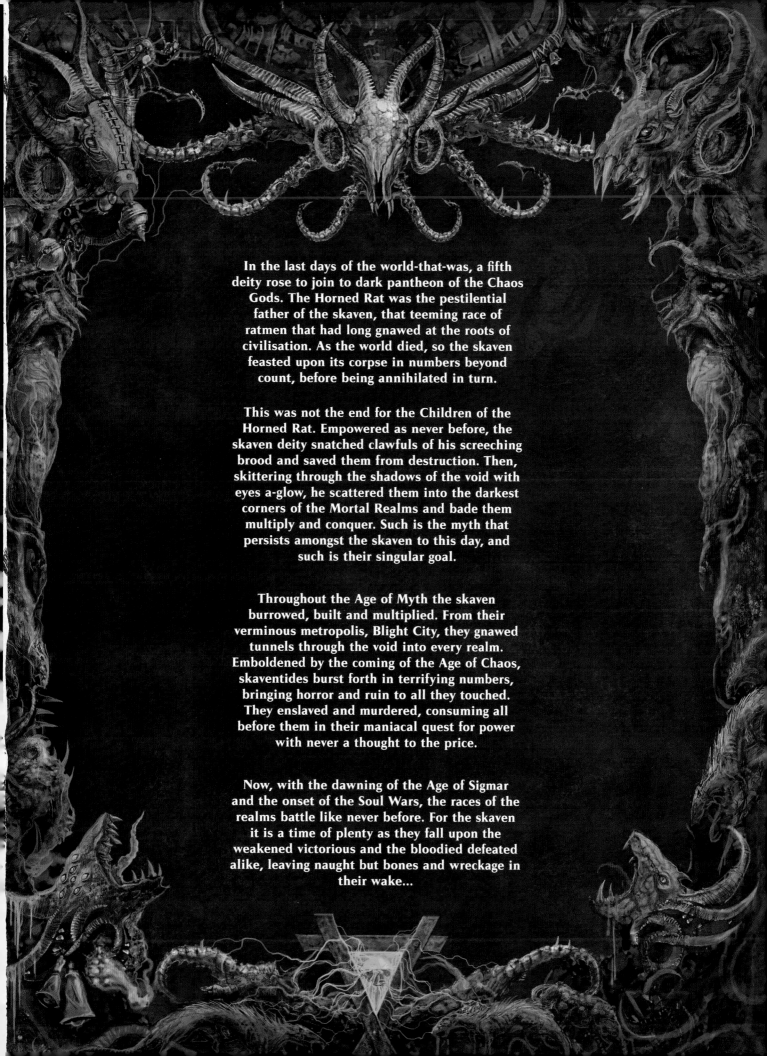

In the last days of the world-that-was, a fifth deity rose to join to dark pantheon of the Chaos Gods. The Horned Rat was the pestilential father of the skaven, that teeming race of ratmen that had long gnawed at the roots of civilisation. As the world died, so the skaven feasted upon its corpse in numbers beyond count, before being annihilated in turn.

This was not the end for the Children of the Horned Rat. Empowered as never before, the skaven deity snatched clawfuls of his screeching brood and saved them from destruction. Then, skittering through the shadows of the void with eyes a-glow, he scattered them into the darkest corners of the Mortal Realms and bade them multiply and conquer. Such is the myth that persists amongst the skaven to this day, and such is their singular goal.

Throughout the Age of Myth the skaven burrowed, built and multiplied. From their verminous metropolis, Blight City, they gnawed tunnels through the void into every realm. Emboldened by the coming of the Age of Chaos, skaventides burst forth in terrifying numbers, bringing horror and ruin to all they touched. They enslaved and murdered, consuming all before them in their maniacal quest for power with never a thought to the price.

Now, with the dawning of the Age of Sigmar and the onset of the Soul Wars, the races of the realms battle like never before. For the skaven it is a time of plenty as they fall upon the weakened victorious and the bloodied defeated alike, leaving naught but bones and wreckage in their wake...

CONTENTS

DESIGNED BY GAMES WORKSHOP IN NOTTINGHAM
With thanks to The Faithful for their additional playtesting services.

Games Workshop Ltd., Willow Road, Lenton, Nottingham, NG7 2WS, United Kingdom
games-workshop.com

A Verminlord Warpseer leads an unstoppable skaven swarm as it surges from the blighted depths to overrun the beleaguered battle lines of Sigmar's Stormcast Eternals.

THE SKAVEN

The skaven are a race of mutant ratmen. They are true beings of Chaos, their every thought turned towards selfish advancement and conquest. Their technologies and magics are powered by the foul substance known as warpstone. Anarchic, prolific and deranged, the skaven are a threat to every living being in the Mortal Realms.

The enemy's first warning is the scrabbling of a million claws and the skin-crawling susurrus of thousands of furry bodies squirming over and around one another. The sound carries up from the dark and noisome depths, mingling with a verminous reek that grows thicker and more cloying by the moment.

Warriors eye one another nervously, gritting their teeth and trying not to edge backwards as the distant rushing grows to a skittering roar. Squealing war cries and spite-filled shrieks echo on the air. Countless red and staring eyes flash in the gloom, and torchlight glints upon chisel fangs and rusted blades. Terrible witch-lights flare to life as the swarm bears down upon its terrified foe, dark sorcery and malign technologies spitting their fury in the instant before the tidal wave of flesh and fur hits home. Then the skaven crash headlong into their enemies and sweep them away in a frenzy of horror and blood.

These humanoid vermin stand perhaps a little shorter than a grown man, their build wiry, their limbs corded with whip-thin muscle and ending in vicious hand- and foot-claws. Their jaws are dominated by wicked incisors, their red eyes glint with vicious cunning and their every movement is jerky and swift, filled with a nervous energy. Skaven are cowardly and selfish creatures, as likely to squirt the musk of fear and flee if faced with a fair fight. However, in large numbers they gain a kind of rabid courage, and when enough ratmen mass into an onrushing skaventide they prove unstoppable.

The skaven are devious and inventive creatures whose weapons and wargear, though unstable, are nevertheless ruinously powerful. Even the least of their Clanrat foot soldiers goes to battle clutching a notched blade and a battered shield, and clad in a patchwork of armour that he has scavenged from his fallen comrades. The true skaven shock troops wield all manner of devastating weaponry, from heavy halberds and long-barrelled rifles to steam-driven rotary cannons, warpstone-fuelled fire throwers and weighty glass globes that release the dreaded poisoned wind when they shatter amongst the foe. Many of these devices are as likely to slay their wielders in spectacular mishaps as they are to slaughter the foe, but to the skaven, life is cheap, and no matter how many hapless underlings must die to achieve it, victory is all that counts.

The skaven do not restrict their callous ingenuity to iron and brass alone. Using the power of warpstone, they twist the flesh of living beings into grotesque new shapes. The skaven craft monsters of wet muscle and jutting fangs that are driven into battle, there to spend their fury and pain upon the enemy before their distorted bodies collapse beneath the weight of their own horrific mutations.

Foul alchemy and all manner of low cunning and trickery combine to make the skaven a foe to inspire fear in the stoutest hearts. Yet their greatest strength lies in their sheer, incalculable numbers. A lone skaven is dangerous but ultimately cowardly and self-serving, unlikely to attack unless its victim is weak, incapacitated or unaware of the threat. When they gather in numbers, however, the skaven

BLIGHT CITY

Built upon bedrock of pure warpstone, sprawling in its fractal enormity beyond the bounds of reality, Blight City is the capital of skavendom. It is the smog-wreathed heart of the Under-Empire, and a more nightmarish warren of industry, poverty and bloodshed is hard to imagine. Blight City is ever-expanding, ever-changing as new warrens and burrows are dug out or collapse, new bell towers, factories, fleshmoulding pits and fortifications rise and fall. The skyline heaves likes the flank of a dying beast. The city's myriad districts rise in layer upon layer of tangled and mouldering architecture, with the new built hastily atop the old until at last the weight of the whole unstable edifice brings entire regions crashing down. Scavengers beyond number pick through the ruins. Slaves and labourers toil in their billions for the glory of their masters. Workshops fizz and spark, vast bells toll, creaking wheels the size of mountains turn to generate power for monstrous machines, and always the clans war from one district to the next, capturing, conquering, razing and enslaving in their turn.

This is the swift-beating and rot-black heart of the skaven Under-Empire. Its trillions-upon-trillions of verminous denizens are forever in conflict, always attempting to scrabble to power over one another's gnawed corpses. Escaped slaves and wild-eyed outcasts fight with huge vermin for scraps in the underwarrens. Lower-ranked clans constantly skirmish, politic and sabotage to ascend the societal rungs, while those higher up the pecking order battle to keep what they have, to undermine their rivals, or to climb higher still. Meanwhile, one skaven army after another scurries out into the realms through pulsating gnawholes, skaventides carrying the corruption of Blight City out to poison the Mortal Realms.

become braver by far. Exhorted into battle by their leaders – who position themselves carefully at the rear of any assault and well out of harm's way – the mad-eyed hordes of the skaven sweep forward in a chittering mass to tear apart all who oppose them.

BORN TO RULE

Every single skaven is a compulsive liar and a megalomaniac, convinced of his own pre-eminence. From the lowliest slave to the most powerful warlord, each one believes that he – and he alone – is the ultimate recipient of the Great Horned Rat's favour. Every skaven sees himself as a genius surrounded by expendable fools, who will eventually rise to command all he surveys and conquer the Mortal Realms in the name of his scabrous deity. It is a trait that propels the skaven to infeasible victory as often as it leads them to catastrophic defeat.

Just as they see themselves as the inevitable inheritors of the Mortal Realms, the skaven view all other sentient beings as degenerate imbeciles. They refer to the members of other races as 'things' – 'man-things', 'aelf-things', 'green-things' – and despise them all for their inability to recognise the skaven as their rightful rulers. Yet there is an inherent contradiction in the skaven, just as there is in their fractured deity. Thus, even as they preen, assured in their superiority, so the skaven suffer from an embittered inferiority complex that drives them to subjugate and torment those they believe to be looking down upon them. Many of these mutant ratmen are paranoid and ever fearful, given to obsessing over the perceived sleights, plotting and scorn that they see in every deed and word of those around them.

Coupled with their utter disregard for any save themselves, this volatile brew of arrogance, conceit and outright delusion makes the skaven unpredictable and dangerous. Every moment of deranged brilliance, every dark flash of inspiration is turned towards fashioning both plans and weapons of conquest. Every second is spent in the furtherance of plots intended to raise the skaven up to glory atop a gnawed mountain of slain enemies and rivals.

That so many of these overly elaborate schemes unravel with disastrous consequences is of little concern to the skaven. Failure can always be blamed upon the incompetence of underlings or the efforts of unseen enemies. So long as one scurries away to fight another day, there is no debacle that cannot be turned into an opportunity, given sufficient deception, manipulation and murder.

UNDER-EMPIRE

The constant struggle for supremacy that characterises skaven society is no chance occurrence. It stems from the Horned Rat himself, who would see his multitudinous brood battle one another until only the swift and the cunning survive. The constant goad of ambition and internecine warfare ensures that the weak and foolish are quickly weeded out and eaten, leaving the deadliest of the skaven race to rise to the top. Through this ceaseless infighting, the Great Horned Rat believes, his seething children will become ever stronger until at last they gnaw away the foundations upon which the other gods' power rests. On that day, when all comes crashing down to final wrack and ruin, it will be the Horned Rat and his brood that emerge to feast upon the corpses and preen victorious atop the mounded dead.

To this end the skaven drive ever outwards. Their capital, Blight City, is the rotten and swift-beating heart of an Under-Empire that stretches across all eight Mortal Realms and into the Realm of Chaos itself. Every day the skaven spread further. Every day they multiply in the dark and noisome shadows of the realms. Every day they burrow out new fortified warrens and invade fresh enemy territories, seeking always the ultimate conquest that they see as their inalienable right.

WARPSTONE

Amongst the most dread substances in all the Mortal Realms is warpstone. A fierce green corona wreathes this night-black crystal, smouldering with the unbridled power of mutation and madness. It is the condensed form of magic that has been fully corrupted by the powers of Chaos, and merely to touch it is to invite insanity, corruption and death. Warpstone eats the light around it, so that it is forever wreathed in an unnatural pall.

Warpstone is coveted by the skaven clans, who use it to fuel their insane inventions and abominable flesh-grafting mutations. While extremely hazardous to work with and prone to sudden, violent explosion, warpstone generates vast amounts of energy if properly tapped. The mightiest of ratman sorcerers even consume the stuff, either as raw chunks or in the form of refined powders sniffed up the snout or rubbed into the gums. This practice imparts bursts of unnatural magical might, though the risks to body and mind are so severe that none but the skaven would even contemplate such an insane deed.

It was thanks to the devious Grey Seer Thanquol that a mighty skaventide gathered and invaded Barak-Nar. Pouring through a gaping gnawhole in the sky-port's lowest bilges, the skaven wrought bloody havoc and countless acts of sabotage before their leaders, Thanquol chief amongst them, vanished as suddenly as they had arrived.

THE HORNED RAT

The skaven deity is a fractured and anarchic being, but a terrifyingly ambitious one. The Horned Rat is a grasping, paranoid abomination who seeks to achieve final primacy amongst the Chaos pantheon through the ruination of the Mortal Realms and the annihilation of all those who worship – and thus empower – his rivals.

The Great Horned Rat gnaws endlessly at the roots of reality. He is a monstrous entity, an ancient god of scavenging hunger and infinite, malevolent cunning. He creeps through the dark spaces behind the physical plane and stares from the shadows with glinting eyes. The whisper of his presence inspires atavistic horror. The scratch of his claws and the drag of his worm-like tail through the void drives seers mad and sends ripples of nightmares roiling through mortal minds.

The other gods underestimate the Great Horned Rat at their peril. Even as their own worshippers fight and die in costly wars of conquest, faith and vengeance, so the Children of the Horned Rat multiply in the shadows at a ferocious rate. It is said that, no matter where one stands in the Mortal Realms, a skaven is never more than a spear's throw away and in this there is a horrible kernel of truth. Skaven gnawholes bore through the bedrock of reality itself at their deity's bidding, even – it is whispered – into heavenly Azyr. Thus, as the servants of the deities of Order, Chaos, Destruction and Death wax and wane in bloody service to their gods, ever the

Horned Rat's brood become more numerous, more powerful and more of a lurking threat to all other life in the Mortal Realms. Only when the time is right will they strike as one, and on that day the Horned Rat will feast upon the corpses of his many vanquished foes.

SPLINTERED ASPECTS

The skaven view their god in many different ways, with each of the Great Clans having their own – wildly varied – depictions of the Horned Rat. To the Clans Verminus, he is the Great Conqueror, the King of Lashes, a warlike and supremely arrogant being who exhorts his worshippers to tear their enemies apart with fang and claw then feast upon their carcasses. To the Clans Pestilens he is the Great Corruptor, a virulent horror of sloughing flesh and rotted bone who desires the Thirteen Great Plagues to be gathered and unleashed upon the Mortal Realms.

The Clans Skryre depict their god as the Dark Innovator, a monster of infernal machineries in whose name they will twist and re-purpose the mechanisms of reality itself, while the Clans Moulder see their

god as the Writhing Broodsire, the Fleshgifter, a protean mass of heaving ratflesh that seeks to see all the realms buried in endlessly ravenous vermin. The Clans Eshin, meanwhile, worship the Horned Rat in his aspect as the Shadow of Murder, the Scuttler-in-the-Walls. In his name they drive their knives into kings, lords and champions, seeking to bring on anarchy through the collapse of just rule.

THE COUNCIL OF THIRTEEN

Ultimate rule of the skaven race lies with the all-powerful Council of Thirteen – or so they believe. Consisting of twelve Lords of Decay and a thirteenth symbolic place reserved for the Horned Rat, this council comprises the rulers of the mightiest clans. The Great Clans each maintain at least one seat on the council, with additional seats divided between them and the Grey Seers. Of all the seats, the first and twelfth are considered pre-eminent, for they are situated to the right and left of the Horned Rat's position.

The council meets in an immense chamber atop the Tower of Kavzar

*D*eep in the bowels of Blight City, a furtive figure scurried from one patch of shadow to the next. Ducking beneath a tangle of old pipework and picking his way between puddles of glowing green ooze, Skretch darted down a narrow side-tunnel. He emerged into a long-forgotten chamber. Here he stopped and threw back his hood, revealing the crest of curling horns that marked him as a Grey Seer. Skretch surveyed the ritual markings that he had scribed across the walls, floor and ceiling of this old burrow. Sweeping curves and jagged lines intersected madly, all glowing a curdled green. Dark power hung in the air, awaiting only a catalyst to surge to malevolent life. Now, Skretch brought that catalyst from beneath his robes; the still-beating heart of his late rival Kwirrik. He lifted the pulsating morsel of flesh and bit into it, blood drizzling over his muzzle as he spat the chewed gore into the centre

of the summoning circle. Green light pulsed, warp lightning flashed, and Skretch felt his glands tighten as something malevolent pushed its way through the veil. The Grey Seer fell to his knees as the monstrous form of a Verminlord unfolded itself to loom over him.

'You dare-dare to summon me, little seer?' asked the daemon. 'Why?'

'Power,' replied Skretch, fighting the urge to grovel. 'A seat on the council, yes-yes. I desire it. I deserve it!'

The Verminlord gave a hissing laugh. For a second Skretch feared the daemon would devour him.

'Very well, little seer,' it said instead, leering. 'Tell-speak what you offer in return.'

Grey Seer Skretch felt a surge of elation and marshalled his thoughts. He had much to offer, he was sure. This daemon would do his bidding, of course, for he was the mighty Skretch! And oh, how his rivals would suffer...

at the heart of Blight City. Known as the Masterburrow, this cavernous space – large enough to permit substantial troop movements should a diplomatic deadlock need to be settled through the use of force – incorporates thirteen sub-towers that line the circular sweep of the walls at regular intervals just outside of effective weapons range – most notably that of the notorious Warplock Jezzails. Each tower supports a grand balcony-dais upon which a Lord of Decay may sit enthroned and screech at his rivals through snoutaphones and amplisqueaker arrays. The Lords of Decay invest vast resources in warding their towers against attempted assassination, be it via magic, conventional weaponry, tailored plagues or assassins' venoms – indeed, they put almost as much effort into their own protection as they do into seeking ways to penetrate the defences of their fellows.

Looking to impress and intimidate, the Lords of Decay further enhance their daises with all manner of elaborate stage-dressing. Lord Hakkrit of Verminus Clan Fang, for example, festoons his dais with heads on spikes and enough banners to fill a military encampment. High Arch-Warlock Skrach of Skryre Clan Ezzik sits within an armoured mechanical simulacrum of himself that stands thirteen feet tall and shoots fire from its snout, while Master Threkk of Eshin Clan Scurrie speaks in eerie whispers that carry from behind a shroud of impenetrable shadow.

Only the ominous Thirteenth Tower stands empty, its dais playing host to an outsized throne fashioned from pure warpstone. This is the symbolic seat of the Horned Rat, and behind it yawns a huge crack in the stonework of the tower whose depths vanish into fathomless darkness. An ill wind gusts from that shadowy void, bringing with it the stench of rank fetor and the distant scratch and scrabble of myriad claws. Those few arrogant or unfortunate skaven who have attempted to enter the crack and explore its depths have never been seen again.

During particularly turbulent periods in the history of the skaven, the terrifying Verminlord known as Skreech Verminking has squirmed from the nameless crack to sit upon the warpstone throne. These are the only times during which the Council of Thirteen is ever truly unified – at least outwardly – for even a Lord of Decay knows better than to denounce the word of the Horned Rat's avatar. The rat daemon has ordered gnawholes bored and invasions unleashed, ended civil wars through bloody example, and set in motion schemes to pit the Lords of Decay against one another. This would appear to be as much direct involvement as the Verminlords have in the rule of the council. Yet in truth, even the Lords of Decay have been deceived.

THE SHADOW COUNCIL

Beyond the warpstone throne, far down the gullet of the yawning crack – that is, in truth, a gnawhole riddled with warding curses no mortal creature could endure – lies a horrifying sub-realm. It is a space of indeterminate size and constantly shifting shadows. Its boundaries are indistinct, resembling one moment a mountain range of stitched and quivering flesh, the next a scrabbling sea of claws and fangs, the next a soaring wall of poisonous fog or an all-consuming expanse of shadow in which glint blood-red eyes. An omnipresent scraping and scritching fills the air, and a sense of watchful menace and suspicion suffuses all. The light shifts from spills of venomous green to stirring masses of grey-black shadow, lit by sudden arcs of lightning. A cold wind blows, moaning low as though it spills through endless mountains of fang-gnawed bones, and a mighty bell tolls far off and ominous.

In this awful place, known to its denizens as the Deepengnaw, the Shadow Council meet to determine the course of skavendom. Thirteen Verminlords make up the Shadow Council, perched upon ruinous daises twisted from living flesh, churning gears and boiling darkness around a vast sigil of the Horned Rat wrought of warpstone and brass. Twelve of the Shadow Council's places are ever in flux, repeatedly seized and lost based upon the rat daemons' metaphysical machinations. The mixture of Verminlord Deceivers, Warbringers, Corruptors, Warpseers and others changes by the day – sometimes by the hour – and each brings their own agendas and desires to the endless debate. The only constant is the thirteenth of their number, Skreech Verminking. Even the other Verminlords – immortal daemonic monstrosities that they are – fear this eldritch creature, for if the Horned Rat himself were to have a strong left claw then Verminking would be it. His words split the air as though the Horned One himself had uttered them, and if his fellows seek to work against him, they do so only behind the greatest veils of secrecy. Even then, such efforts are rarely successful, nearly always ending in ghastly tragedy for all concerned.

Though the Shadow Council interpret the Horned Rat's will, they rarely pass their direction on to the mortal skaven directly. Such candour is not in their nature. Instead they influence and manipulate from behind the scenes. Some Verminlords whisper into Grey Seers' minds, filling them with ambitions and schemes that they cannot differentiate from their own. Others appoint themselves as patrons to particular skaven leaders, be they existing Lords of Decay or those who would take their places. Still others – especially the Verminlord Warpseers – act through entire networks of ratspaws, or – in the case of many Warbringers and Deceivers – manifest in the Mortal Realms to take direct action.

Thus, even as the Council of Thirteen try to advance their own clans and ambitions, so the Shadow Council work at their own multifarious plots, and the whole vast engine of agendas, cruelty, paranoia and nepotism grinds countless skaven lives in its gears. Such is the essential nature of this eternally fractured race and – so long as his children continue to multiply and to conquer – the Horned Rat is content to watch it all play out.

Twisted and splintered are the many aspects of the Horned Rat, each godhead a baleful reflection of this dark and verminous deity's monstrous whole.

WAR BETWEEN THE CLANS

Skaven society is made up of clans, each of which derives from one of the five Great Clans. Named Verminus, Skryre, Pestilens, Eshin and Moulder, each of these Great Clans has its own distinct areas of expertise and ways of making war, and each is wholly convinced that they – and they alone – should rule skavendom.

So swiftly do the skaven multiply, and so widespread are they throughout the Mortal Realms that it is impossible to gauge their true strength. Were the Lords of Decay to be asked how many skaven they ruled, their most seemingly hyperbolic boast would likely fall short of the truth. Even the Horned Rat himself struggles to keep track of all his swarming brood, but suffice it to say that there are probably more skaven in the Mortal Realms than there are grains of sand in all the dismal deserts of Shyish.

It is unsurprising, therefore, that there are billions of skaven clans. Some, the especially far flung or nascent, may number only a few dozen ratmen led by a particularly scurrilous and ambitious claw-leader. By comparison, the largest clans comprise teeming millions of skaven, their tunnels and burrows honeycombing entire regions of the realms. Yet no matter how large or small a clan is, no matter how individually powerful its rulers,

they all owe fealty to one of the Great Clans.

Throughout skaven history, the Great Clans have vied constantly for pre-eminence, their efforts helped or hampered by the ever-meddling Order of Grey Seers, also known as the Masterclan. When a Great Clan is in the ascendant, its clans are commensurately more influential, feared and resented, and its methods for advancing skavendom come to the fore.

When the Clans Verminus rule the Council of Thirteen, for example, skaven armies typically rely upon sheer weight of numbers to secure victory and become more warlike and expansionist, often boasting huge spearheads of Stormvermin. Should Eshin come to the fore, the skaven swarms become more reliant upon secrecy, cunning and assassination. Scars have been left upon the collective skaven psyche by those horrific periods during which the deranged fleshcrafters of the

Clans Moulder ruled the council. Few – barring Moulder themselves of course – are keen to see their return. Since the dawn of the Age of Sigmar, it has been the Clans Pestilens and Skryre who have vied for a commanding share of seats on the Council of Thirteen.

IRON AND FILTH

The Clans Skryre employ equal parts dark science, unholy alchemy and magic in the creation of their machines. They are prolific – if anarchic – innovators and engineers. The Horned Rat blessed them with the relentless drive to invent and experiment, and through costly trial and error their warlocks have developed countless machineries upon which skavendom now greatly depends.

Temperamental farsqueaker machines that allow skaven to communicate over impossible distances, gyre engines that provide power – albeit sporadically –

*T*he sounds of violence echoed up the rocky walls of the ravine. Warlock Engineer Reeknik of Clan Ekkit stood atop the cliff edge – not too close, lest an ambitious underling give him an accidental shove – and looked down upon the carnage below. The ravine was packed from its eastern end by a savage mass of Bonesplitter orruks, drums thundering and voices raised in savage chants. Pouring in from the opposite end and meeting the greenskins in bloody battle were the Plague Monks of Clan Sputix. Ragged skaven surged in their hundreds against the orruk battle line, shrieking and squealing as they stabbed with poisoned blades. Bells and gongs raised a discordant clangour, and poisonous fumes from dozens of plague censers wreathed the battle.

Through his warp-optics, Reeknik could see his temporary ally, the Plague Priest Skrokk, leading the fight from atop his Plague Furnace. Alone, neither clan had been a match for the greenskins infesting this region, but together they had the strength and cunning to prevail. Thus, after much posturing and numerous threats, the skaven leaders had managed to agree a plan. The Plague Monks would lure the

Bonesplitterz into the ravine, before the war engines of Clan Ekkit fired from on high to break their strength. Reeknik surveyed his Warp Lightning Cannons, lined up along the lip of the ravine. It was almost too easy, he thought, then puffed up his chest and screeched his orders.

'Fire! Shoot-shoot! Kill-slay the green things and the Clan Sputix both!'

Chittering with wicked laughter, his crews pulled firing levers to unleash a rain of death upon the combatants below. Most were still leering in amusement when the plague-bombs – wired into the Skryre firing mechanisms by Gutter Runner saboteurs in the pay of Plague Priest Skrokk – detonated. The Ekkit batteries vanished in a roiling cloud of corrosive smog that rusted brass and iron in seconds, and reduced Reeknik and his underlings to bubbling slicks of rotting flesh before they could even scream.

In the ravine below, Plague Priest Skrokk glanced up with an evil grin as he saw the lethal cloud erupt along the Skryre firing line. He didn't need those cog-snouts, he thought madly as skaven and orruks fought and died all around him. The Clan Sputix was invincible!

throughout Blight City, iconic war engines such as the Warp Lightning Cannon or the Doomwheel; from mountain-sized machineries to minute gadgets no larger than a claw or fang, the Clans Skryre build them all and sell them on to whichever clans can afford their exorbitant prices.

Skryre armies are packed with lethal machines of destruction and Acolytes manning unpredictable but terrifyingly potent wonder-weapons. Often less numerous than the swarms of the other Great Clans, Skryre forces nonetheless can spew out more than enough arcane firepower to slaughter enemy armies many times their number, and are forever pushing out through the Mortal Realms on acquisitive missions to secure knowledge and materials for their cruel and arrogant masters.

Where Skryre rely on iron and cogs, the Clans Pestilens pursue a more biological approach to warfare. They are purveyors of plague and distillers of disease. Their Congregations of Filth flow across the realms wreathed in virulent miasmas, and they do everything in their power to spread the effects of their many poxes far and wide. To the Clans Pestilens the Horned Rat is the Great Corruptor, and in his name they seek to gather the metaphysical ingredients for the Thirteen Great Plagues. By unleashing these cataclysmic diseases, they believe that they will bring everything to final ruination, over which their scavenger deity will reign supreme.

PATHS TO POWER

The balance of power between the Great Clans shifts constantly. From politicking to assassination, bare-faced lying to open armed conflict, the Lords of Decay baulk at nothing so long as it will advance their personal agendas. It is the rare gift of such truly great skaven to be able to see further than the next few hours or days, and to lay accordingly ambitious and convoluted plans. One thing increases the strength and influence of a Great Clan more than anything else, however: successful conquests in the Mortal Realms and – through them – the acquisition of territory and resources in the Horned Rat's name. In this, both the Clans Pestilens and the Clans Skryre have been especially successful in recent years.

When the Age of Chaos began, Nurgle – the Chaos God of plagues – invaded Ghyran. His Maggotkin legions marched upon the holdings of Alarielle the Everqueen and hundreds of the Clans Pestilens scurried alongside them. The Clans Pestilens and the followers of Nurgle make natural allies, for both use disease as a weapon and both factions are – more or less – immune to the horrifying sicknesses and chaotic taint of the other. Thousands upon thousands of Congregations of Filth flowed into battle alongside daemonic Tallybands and Rotbringer Cysts, and wherever they struck they brought about the withering of all that their Sylvaneth foes held dear.

For all their similarities, however, Nurgle and the Great Corruptor are very different deities with very different goals. Where Nurgle delights in the cycle of disease, decay and burgeoning – if revolting – new life, the Horned Rat wants only ruin. The worshippers of Nurgle saw the Clans Pestilens as short-sighted, self-aggrandising little monsters good only for shock troops and cannon fodder. The Plague Monks, meanwhile, sneered down their snouts at Nurgle's servants, viewing them as slow, lumpen oafs whose efforts at ruination were constantly undone by their own excessive sentimentality.

Despite their differences, the chaotic forces knew victory after victory in the War of Life. Yet with the coming of the Age of Sigmar, and the rebirth of the Everqueen Alarielle in her war aspect, conquest turned to catastrophe.

Typically for skaven, the Clans Pestilens took their allies' defeats and turned them to their own advantage. They surged into abandoned Dreadholds and claimed them in the name of the Great Corruptor. They pinned failures upon the ineptitude of their erstwhile Maggotkin allies. They fell upon Sylvaneth and Rotbringers alike where they were exhausted from battling one another, and even burrowed hidden lairs beneath newly founded citadels of Order, there to lurk and fester until the time was right to strike again. So did the Clans Pestilens rapidly increase their standing within the Council of Thirteen.

By comparison, the Clans Skryre have advanced themselves through technological innovation and vast wealth. Some believe that the Clans Skryre had heard whispers of Sigmar's armies gathering in the Heavens, that perhaps the Arch-Warlocks had agents or devices that gave them eyes inside Azyr itself. Whatever the truth, when the Stormhosts descended and the Age of Sigmar began the Clans Skryre were ready. They revealed an array of wonder-weapons and perfected machineries of death that could be employed to turn back even a Stormcast assault – for the right price in warptokens, of course. Yet as their power built, the Clans Skryre also employed their weapons in new wars of conquest of their own. They sought a very specific prize: realmstone.

The Mortal Realms are replete with natural magics. Where these energies gather in especially high concentrations they coalesce into realmstone. From the gossamer tangles of lies given form that are Ulguan realmstone, to the macabre grave-sand of Shyish or the burning primordial coal of Aqshyan emberstone, each Mortal Realm has its own very different form of realmstone. Yet in all cases they are sources of such phenomenal power that – if tapped by the unwary – they can bring horror and catastrophe on all around them.

Until recent years, there had been little call for the skaven to employ

realmstone, as Blight City sat upon vast reserves of warpstone. Rumour had it that the Clans Eshin made limited use of the realmstone of Ulgu in some of their most potent charms and weapons, but other than that the Children of the Horned Rat disdained it as inferior to warpstone.

Then came Arch-Warlock Skrach of Clan Ezzik. Young, aggressive and possessed of a breadth of vision rare among his species, Skrach – then but an Acolyte with ideas above his station – succeeded in refining a minute quantity of Chamonite transmutational gold and using it to supercharge a Warp Lightning Cannon. When that cannon was subsequently employed to annihilate Retch-Chanter Bubolskrit and his entire coven of Plague Priests, Acolyte Skrach ascended to the rank of Warlock Engineer. He began gathering resources to seek out and capture more realmstone. It was his vision that the Clans Skryre would harness magical energies that no other Great Clan understood, and through them would ascend to absolute power over skavendom. Secretly, Skrach harboured dreams of overthrowing Archaon the Everchosen, and becoming the new favoured champion of Chaos with the Horned Rat as his almighty patron.

Megalomaniac though he was, Skrach was no fool. Within a decade he had clambered up a mountain of slain test-victims, rivals and erstwhile allies to seize one of the most powerful seats on the Council of Thirteen. Now, more than ever, High Arch-Warlock Skrach seeks out deposits of realmstone. He looks to fathom ways that their power can be harnessed and blended with warpstone to create even more powerful energy sources. Should he succeed on the scale he envisions, all the Mortal Realms will tremble at the might of the Clans Skryre.

A PRECARIOUS BALANCE

At the end of the Realmgate Wars it was arguable that the Clans Skryre and the Clans Pestilens were both poised to seize dominance of skavendom. In terms of martial might it was the Clans Pestilens that posed the greater threat. However, much of that strength was still committed to the war in Ghyran. By comparison, the Clans Skryre had consolidated their power base in Blight City itself, even daring to raise ratling cannon towers and warp-rocket batteries within striking distance of the Tower of Kavzar itself. The implicit threat was obvious to all, its arrogance astounding.

Then came the Shyish necroquake. This catastrophic event was the culmination of the Great Necromancer Nagash's plan to exterminate all living beings in the Mortal Realms and raise them as his undying servitors. Instead, thanks to the meddling of the Clans Eshin, Nagash's great endeavour raged out of control and sent untrammelled magics pulsing across the Mortal Realms. The dead rose in their billions, untamed spells prowled the lands like predatory beasts. Catastrophic destruction was unleashed.

Located as it is beyond the bounds of reality, Blight City was shielded from the worst effects of the necroquake. Still, massive shock waves rolled through the endless sprawl and sent entire warren-districts crashing down in ruin. Terror spread as invasions of screaming ghasts burst into the city through open gnawholes, and war lit the tangled streets aflame as the skaven fought back the invaders.

Every opportunist in Blight City sought to take advantage of the mayhem to advance their own cause, with the Lords of Decay chief amongst them. Even before the dust had settled it became clear that no fewer than four Lords of Decay had been slain or had vanished, leading to rapid appointments of successors and swift, violent manoeuvrings for power. For a matter of days, the Clans Pestilens held a commanding three seats on the council, but the alarmed backlash of assassinations this triggered soon saw the council's fifth seat left empty and hotly contested. At the same time the Clans Skryre were prevented from 'securing' the council chambers only through a mixture of vicious politicking and overt military intervention by the Masterclan and several Clans Verminus.

The Council of Thirteen find themselves in as precarious a position as they have seen for centuries. Both Skryre and Pestilens agitate for all-out civil war, their posturing and aggression becoming more pronounced by the day. Verminus and Moulder throw their weight behind first one faction then another, scrabbling for short-term advancement wherever the opportunity presents itself, and the Masterclan frantically manipulate in the hopes of unifying the council again – under their rule, of course. Only Eshin remain aloof, though of course, behind a veil of shadows, they are just as viciously active as their rival Great Clans. The matter must be decided soon, for war rages across the realms as never before and presents countless opportunities for skaven conquest. Yet day by day the unrest triggered by the Clans Skryre and Pestilens worsens.

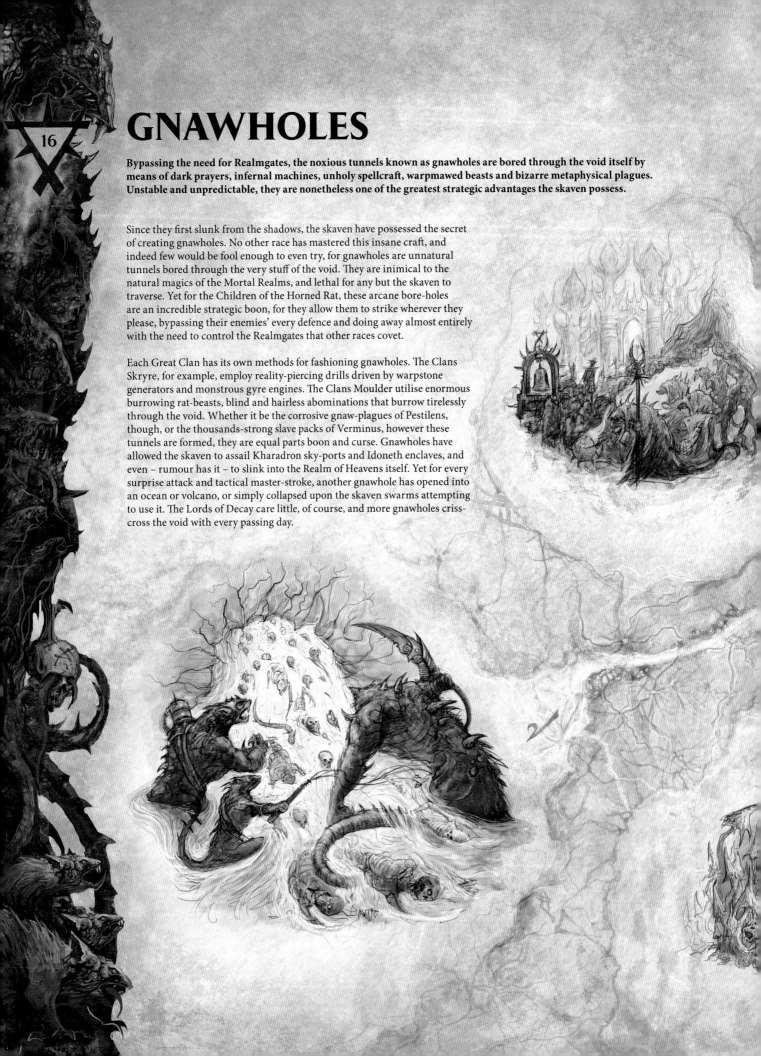

GNAWHOLES

Bypassing the need for Realmgates, the noxious tunnels known as gnawholes are bored through the void itself by means of dark prayers, infernal machines, unholy spellcraft, warpmawed beasts and bizarre metaphysical plagues. Unstable and unpredictable, they are nonetheless one of the greatest strategic advantages the skaven possess.

Since they first slunk from the shadows, the skaven have possessed the secret of creating gnawholes. No other race has mastered this insane craft, and indeed few would be fool enough to even try, for gnawholes are unnatural tunnels bored through the very stuff of the void. They are inimical to the natural magics of the Mortal Realms, and lethal for any but the skaven to traverse. Yet for the Children of the Horned Rat, these arcane bore-holes are an incredible strategic boon, for they allow them to strike wherever they please, bypassing their enemies' every defence and doing away almost entirely with the need to control the Realmgates that other races covet.

Each Great Clan has its own methods for fashioning gnawholes. The Clans Skryre, for example, employ reality-piercing drills driven by warpstone generators and monstrous gyre engines. The Clans Moulder utilise enormous burrowing rat-beasts, blind and hairless abominations that burrow tirelessly through the void. Whether it be the corrosive gnaw-plagues of Pestilens, though, or the thousands-strong slave packs of Verminus, however these tunnels are formed, they are equal parts boon and curse. Gnawholes have allowed the skaven to assail Kharadron sky-ports and Idoneth enclaves, and even – rumour has it – to slink into the Realm of Heavens itself. Yet for every surprise attack and tactical master-stroke, another gnawhole has opened into an ocean or volcano, or simply collapsed upon the skaven swarms attempting to use it. The Lords of Decay care little, of course, and more gnawholes criss-cross the void with every passing day.

RISE OF THE UNDER-EMPIRE

The history of the skaven is an anarchic tangle of lies, half-truths and exaggerations in which every ratman believes himself the hero and all others fools. From epic events to distorted fiction, all skaven seek to claim responsibility for their race's victories.

● AGE OF MYTH ●

THE FIRST CLANS

At the dawning of the Age of Myth, the Great Horned Rat slinks from the shadows of the void. In his jaws he holds the first skaven, and these he scatters throughout the darkest corners of the Mortal Realms. These are the first Great Clans, and it is claimed that as many as thirteen were released into the realms, along with the Grey Seers who would guide them. The Great Horned Rat charges his myriad children to multiply, to consume and to ruin, and so they do with frenzied vigour.

BLIGHT CITY FOUNDED

Even while Sigmar is still forming his pantheon, the skaven establish Blight City in a twisted sub-realm lodged like a splinter in the void. Legends differ as to how this occurs. Some say that it is the ruin of a former mighty skaven metropolis, its carcass fetched up upon a vast deposit of warpstone like a wrecked ship impaled upon rocks. Others claim that it begins as a proud city of men and duardin known as Kavzar, that falls prey to the Horned Rat's terrible curse. Every Great Clan proclaims that they, and they alone, founded Blight City, though of course the truth of such assertions will never be known.

GNAWING DOOM

By the teachings of the Verminlords, the skaven gain the ability to create gnawholes. Each Great Clan is quick to take these incantations and arcane secrets and twist them in their own fashion, eagerly 'improving' upon what they have been taught as is the skaven way. From this day onwards, reality will become ever more honeycombed with the winding tunnels of the skaven.

TICHRITT'S DEMISE

The Clans Tichritt, one of the twelve Great Clans that exist at this time, gather their entire strength and launch a vast invasion of Thandria. So confident are they in their superiority of numbers and the power of their chronomantic weapons that they openly defy Sigmar and all his allies. Though more than half of the so-called Endless Kingdom is annihilated by the efforts of the Clans Tichritt, the God-King and his allies crush the skaven and purge them from existence. The eleven Great Clans that remain learn a seminal lesson of caution from the demise of their arrogant cousins.

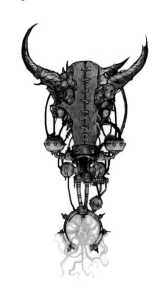

● AGE OF CHAOS ●

RATS IN THE WALLS

During the early invasions of the Age of Chaos, several Slinktalons from Eshin Clan Nichtus aid in the attack upon the immense fortress of Obstryx. Creeping through the fortress' defences while the legions of Slaanesh batter away from outside, the Eshin operatives slay sentries, evade patrols and lace a mile-long section of the walls with gnawbombs. The resultant implosive blast gouges a mighty breach through which the howling Slaaneshi hosts pour to victory. It is a triumph their leader, Prince Sylacitous, never gets to see. He falls to the strike of a Verminlord Deceiver in the last moments before the Eshin operatives vanish without trace, their sudden breaking of faith remaining inexplicable to their former allies.

PARADISE ROTS

As the Age of Chaos begins, Verminlord Corruptor Vermalanx leads a coven of thirteen ancient Plague Priests in a hideous ritual within the Vitreous Vale. Reality itself rots away before their foul magics, spilling raw Chaos into that ancient and beautiful Sylvaneth greenhold.

THE GREAT CIVIL WAR

The bastions of Order fall on every front. As the hordes of Chaos wreak havoc and ruin across the Mortal Realms, the Under-Empire grows fat upon the spoils. Two Great Clans, warlike Verminus and savage Ikk, make the greatest gains during this period, at one point holding an unimaginable four seats each upon the Council of Thirteen. Civil war is inevitable as the two Great Clans vie to seize absolute power, and the remaining seven Great Clans hasten to ally themselves with one side or the other while – in truth – plotting to bring down both. For twenty-six years the war rages, leaving swathes of Blight City ablaze and costing the skaven terribly in lives and territory.

At last, the Clans Verminus enlist the aid of the Clans Pestilens to spread the frothjaw plague through the Clans Ikk, turning their animal ferocity into something uncontrollable and, ultimately, lethal. Over the next two years, the devolving abominations that were once the Clans Ikk run amok through skavendom, but eventually they are annihilated. Their demise leaves a power vacuum and, though the Clans Verminus ostensibly emerge from the civil war as victors, still the conflict rages on.

WAR OF LIFE

While much of skavendom fritter away more than two decades locked in a war of mutual annihilation, many of the Clans Pestilens instead turn their attentions to Ghyran and the War of Life. Virulent Processions pour across the Jade Kingdoms, billions of Plague Monks lending their frenzied fury to Nurgle's onslaught against Alarielle and her Sylvaneth. The Clans Feesik, Morbidus and Septik all gain great power from this ongoing conflict, their sub-sects and thrall clans multiplying again and again to infest ever more of the Realm of Life.

PARASITE ENGINES

A Verminlord Warbringer known as Gnawsoul triggers the invasion of the Scabrous Sprawl in Ghyran. Arch-Warlock Warpskreech leads the attack, unleashing city-sized walking fortresses known as parasite engines that leech the vitality of the lands. This entire invasion, which causes untold devastation and comes with a monstrous cost in lives, is in fact a bid by the Clans Skryre to undermine Pestilens' monopoly in Ghyran while accruing more might for their own ongoing efforts in the Great Civil War.

VERMINKING'S DECREE

Skreech Verminking comes forth to find the Masterburrow itself shuddering in the grip of civil war. Unleashing a horrific curse that blasts the warring clawpacks to ash, he settles himself upon the warpstone throne and glowers at the terrified Lords of Decay. The Great Horned Rat has been amused by his children's squabbles, says Verminking, but now the Great Civil War must end. The other Chaos Gods have waxed in power during the Age of Chaos but the skaven deity has lagged behind as his servants have fought amongst themselves.

Skreech demands that the six surviving Great Clans follow the guidance of the Masterclan from this day forth, and strike not at one another but at the remaining bastions of Order and the servants of the other Dark Gods alike. To ensure obedience, he reduces Arch-Warlock Snitterkrit, Great Plague-speaker Ebolox, Grand Clawlord Thrakk, Things-twister Rukhtik, Lieweaver Yrkrit and Shadowmaster Pheng to sloughing rot and bubbling slime with a twitch of his tail. The surviving Lords of Decay, and those who seize the thrones of the slain, scurry to obey Lord Verminking's decree.

INTO THE BEYOND

As though at some silent call, the Clans Shrykt gather in Aqshy, in the howling caverns. There they dig an almighty gnawhole. They vanish into its depths clan by clan until at last it collapses behind them. No further sign of the Clans Shrykt has been seen since this day, and no skaven has ever determined where they went, nor why.

WATCHING EYES

Barricaded within the Realm of Heavens, hidden behind the most powerful occluding magics ever conjured, Sigmar gathers his Stormcast Eternals. He prepares to unleash a war of reconquest that will drive back the forces of Chaos and shake the Mortal Realms to their cores. Even mighty Tzeentch, the Chaos God of Fate, does not suspect the nature nor the scale of Sigmar's plans. Yet, eyes glinting in the deepest shadows of the God-King's throne room, Eshin operatives watch the final preparations. Quietly they slip away, bearing their priceless knowledge through a well-hidden gnawhole to warn their mysterious masters. The tide is about to turn. The forces of Chaos are about to suffer the greatest blow they have known in a thousand years. The skaven, surely, can capitalise upon this…

● AGE OF SIGMAR ●

SPLITFANG'S END

Clawlord Splitfang finally conquers a ruined duardin karak that he has long contested with Eshin Clan Stryk. Attributing the assassins' sudden retreat to them finally having recognised his absolute supremacy, Splitfang and his Clan Skrabb sweep through the fortress and make it theirs. Just days later, the sealed Realmgate atop the karak mountain blasts open and a force of Astral Templars storm forth. Clawlord Splitfang is slain by Lord-Celestant Proudhelm, Clan Skrabb are overwhelmed by this terrifying new foe and their ragged survivors are rounded up and dragged away into slavery by Clan Stryk's operatives.

WAR IN THE REALMS

All across the Mortal Realms, skaven clans have their schemes soured and their strongholds smashed by the onslaught of the Stormcast Eternals. In the Scabrous Sprawl, Arch-Warlock Warpskreech finds his parasite engines besieged by the Knights Excelsior, the conflict becoming bloodier by the day. In Ghyran, Plague Priest Kratsik of the Red Boil and his Virulent Procession are overrun by a combined force of Sylvaneth and Hallowed Knights before they can unleash their rotsmog upon the Jade Kingdoms. The 'lightning-things' are soon hated and feared in equal measure by many in skavendom. Yet there are those clans who receive forewarning, thanks in large part to favourable connections with one or other of the Clans Eshin, and who are able to melt away before the Stormcasts attack, or launch ambushes of their own.

THE GREAT SCRYING

A message filters through the strata of skavendom, spreading from one Grey Seer to the next via farsqueakers, couriers, scuttleclaw envoys and other, weirder vectors. Travelling alone and in secret, or else at the head of duped or manipulated swarms, the whole order of Grey Seers gathers in Hysh. Their gnawholes bring them to the echoing Chasm of Shattered Questions, where they abandon their bodyguards and surviving protectors and scurry on into the depths. As they do so, Verminlords unfold themselves from the shadows and follow them down, the threat of these fearsome rat daemons more than enough to ward away even the most suicidally curious underling. For thirteen nights and thirteen days, the chasm glows with unholy green witchlights as the Masterclan meets in its entirety. When the Grey Seers emerge again they do so with fresh purpose burning in their eyes.

THE BEASTS OF UHLMARSH

Master Moulder Skabgut unleashes his Fleshmeld Menagerie upon the defenders of Uhlmarsh. Wave upon wave of giant rats and rampaging Rat Ogors are driven back from the stockades by brave Freeguild soldiery. Then the ground within the fortress buckles, bulging upwards then collapsing into a slimy pit. Amidst the rising fumes and billowing smoke, a trio of ghastly Hell Pit Abominations surges up into the stronghold. The massacre that follows is horrific, and leaves Uhlmarsh nothing more than a gore-splattered shell.

THE BUBOE WARS

What begins as a rabid quarrel between two Plague Priests rapidly escalates into a full-blown civil war. Soon the Clans Septik, Virulox and their many sub-clans are tearing one another to pieces all through the fire-lit labyrinth of Pyropia. Virulox develop bizarre new plague engines with the aid of Skryre Clan Phrikk, while Septik seal clawpacts with the Clans Moulder. The war escalates by the day, spilling over into nearby Moonclan lurklairs as it does so.

THE MUCH-GREAT SKY-KILL AIR ARMADA

Inspired by captured Kharadron technologies, Arch-Warlock Steelklaw begins a truly ambitious project. For almost two years, the laboratory burrows of Skryre Clan Shyvik glow with strange lights and swarm with furious industry. At last, the newly self-titled Warlock-Admiral Steelklaw launches his fleet of Skryre airships. Built around cannibalised Kharadron craft and the fevered designs that have poured from Steelklaw's mind, dozens of armoured dirigibles, lightning-ships, warpfire barges and klawbombers take to the skies. Over the months that follow, the skaven sky-pirates of Steelklaw's Much-great Sky-kill Air Armada raid Barak-Zilfin and Barak-Mhornar, annihilate Waaagh! Gutcrusha with bombing from on high, and bring their upstart rivals of Skryre Clan Ziknak to their knees. It is not long before Steelklaw's plans are stolen, copied and spread far and wide, and further skaven armadas begin to menace the skies.

A FITTING END

When wasting pox spreads through their war packs, Moulder Clan Ghrubbitus suffer a severe defeat in their underground war with the Fyreslayers of the Kharzmid lodge. Apoplectic, Master Moulder Skhorj employs torture, intimidation and parasitic spy-beasts to discover that the pox was introduced into his breeding stock by his hated rival, Pontifex-Pestilent Rhaspfang of Pestilens Clan Vomix. Shortly afterwards, Rhaspfang disappears amidst mysterious circumstances. He is never seen again, but when the swarms of Clan Ghrubbitus renew their assault on the Kharzmid's magmahold it is with an especially disease-bloated and horribly disfigured war beast thrashing and screaming at the forefront of their attack.

ANVILHEIM DEVOURED

The Anvils of the Heldenhammer lead a war of reconquest that purges the Slaves to Darkness from the kingdom of Ulhor. Little do they know that, though the taint of Chaos may be gone from the surface, the skaven war burrow of Lurkspine Deeps remains below the surface. The ratmen bide their time, watching with avaricious eyes as the forces of Order raise a rich city – Anvilheim – above their tunnels.

Thirteen years to the day after the first foundations of Anvilheim are laid, the skaventide pours up from below. Verminus Claw-hordes storm up through culverts and sewers to spill through the streets. Plague smog billows, gas-masked Skryre Acolytes dashing through it to hurl their poisonous bombs at the city's reeling defenders. The Anvils of the Heldenhammer, the Freeguilds and Ironweld, even the Order of Azyr all make spirited attempts to drive the skaven back, but they are surrounded, outnumbered and caught completely by surprise. When a coven of Grey Seers summons Skreech Verminking himself to lead the final assault, the defenders of Anvilheim are doomed.

DEATH OF A HERO

After eighteen years of courageous crusading, the aelven drakelord Sethril Brightblade returns to Azyrheim in triumph. He is feted through the streets for his generalship and personal heroism in the war to rid the jungles of Shasmodach of skaven. Brightblade has seen many horrors, endured much personal loss and agony, yet his is a tale of triumph and courage that is trumpeted to the skies by the Grand Assembly of Azyrheim. He is a poster-child for the war to reclaim the realms, and much beloved by all. The shock and horror is so much the greater, then, when Sethril Brightblade is found the morning after his victory parade slumped dead in a chair in his locked quarters atop the high and well-guarded Tower of Triumphs. Brightblade is eyeless, his veins clotted black with poison, the rune of the Clans Eshin carved into his chest and a look of abject horror twisting his features.

STORMTHIEVES

Grey Seer Kritch enlists the aid of Skryre Clan Shokryk for a secretive project. Utilising rumbling, tracked voltovore engines, the skaven attempt to snatch departing Stormcast souls from the air during battle and trap them in Kritch's so-called 'storm-thing snatchers'. Initial experiments prove disastrous when the Celestial Vindicators of Lord-Exorcist Esmodire slaughter Kritch's hireling Clanrats and the only soul drawn into a voltovore engine overloads it and blows it sky-high before flashing back to the Heavens. Yet Kritch and his warlock followers are unperturbed and – chalking their failure up to incompetent underlings – they begin construction on new, more powerful engines that they are sure will do the job.

INEVITABLE VENGEANCE

Several chambers of Stormcast Eternals purge Rotstump Warren in the Jade Kingdom of Veridian. Outraged at the damage done to his web of plots, the Verminlord Corruptor Pestifrious vows vengeance upon those who led the attack. The daemon stalks his prey, spending untold skaven lives to see his foes sicken and die. That Sigmar's heroes can be reforged time and again only deepens and prolongs Pestifrious' furious vendetta.

YEAR OF THE DROWNED RAT

In Shyish, the Realm of Death, Nagash nears completion of his Great Black Pyramid. Raised at the heart of his capital, Nagashizzar, this cyclopean edifice will unleash the unstoppable energies of death magic upon the Mortal Realms and annihilate all life. Determined to prevent this occurrence, the Lords of Decay scramble to launch multiple assaults against Nagashizzar. The greatest of these is a millions-strong swarm led by the preening Master Moulder Things-master Snitterskritch. However, the Things-master's glorious assault is brought to a premature and ignominious halt when his gnawhole emerges at the bottom of the Kaphtar Sea. A zombie-choked flood tide thunders down the tunnel, a crushing sledgehammer of dark waters that kills Snitterskritch and his swarms before erupting in a mile-high geyser in Blight City. Slitwarren, the Gyredelve and Scuttlebleak are all flooded. A vast infestation of Deadwalkers pushes out into the neighbouring districts, the reanimated corpses of Snitterskritch and his warriors amongst them.

THE CORPSE-THING WAR

Though several secondary invasion swarms continue to move against Nagashizzar, the Council of Thirteen now turn their full horrified attention to the Floodwarrens and undead hordes spilling into the heart of Blight City. The districts afflicted are only a handful of miles from the Tower of Kavzar, and many clans scramble to hurl their warriors at the invading foe. More scurry rapidly out of harm's way, Skryre engineers fleeing with their prized inventions and leaving their underlings to drown or be torn apart by hundreds of groaning zombies. Skirmishes break out amongst the defending forces as some clans attempt to capitalise upon territory lost or abandoned by their rivals, while others pull out of clawpacts at the last moment and allow their supposed allies to be overrun, only to find themselves outnumbered and dragged down in turn. For several perilous days the threat draws ever closer to the Masterburrow, and the Lords of Decay are reduced to outraged screeching and violent recrimination as their every plan to stop the invaders fails. Then comes Grey Seer Thanquol. To some he is a stranger and an upstart, to others a name out of half-remembered myth. To most, he appears an egomaniacal lunatic. However, somehow – accounts vary and confusion reigns as to his precise methods – Thanquol orchestrates a series of ever-more convoluted attacks by scrabbled-together swarms that first blunt and then drive back the undead. After several more days of desperate conflict, the threat is contained and Thanquol disappears as suddenly as he appeared. He does so driven by justified paranoia that the Council of Thirteen will want to quickly crush such a successful leader, and that a large number of very unhappy Clawlords will want to 'discuss' the catastrophic cost in skaven lives that his plans entailed.

NECROQUAKE

Tempted by the promise of a wealth of Shyishan realmstone, Grey Seer Retchnik allies himself with Eshin Clan Slynk and contrives a way for their agents to creep down the part-flooded gnawhole, through the bed of the Kaphtar Sea and into Nagashizzar. Neither Retchnik nor the Eshin agents survive the machinations that surround this alliance, but their meddling ensures that – as Nagash triggers his Great Black Pyramid – hapless Eshin agents are trapped within it. Their presence sours the ritual and causes it to rage out of control. The necroquake is unleashed. The dead rise in their trillions across the Mortal Realms. Endless spells are set loose to prey upon friend and foe alike. It is a matter of hours before the skaven begin to fight amongst themselves to claim credit for this clearly masterful and obviously entirely intentional act of sabotage…

SORCERY UNLEASHED

At the battle of Six Twistings, Pestilens Clan Shrok unleash the Neverplague upon their Sylvaneth foes. Not to be outdone, Grey Seer Krektus summons first a Warp Lightning Vortex and then the terrifying Bell of Doom. While the spinning warp crystals whirl around the Sylvaneth and blast them with furious lightnings, the eldritch bell tolls again and again, sending shock waves of madness and terror through the plague-ridden forest spirits. Soon enough, their battle line collapses altogether and Krektus' swarm ends the day gnawing upon their shattered lamentiri.

DEATH IN THE DEEPS

A fleet of strange submersibles launched by the Clans Skryre begins a bloody invasion of the Idoneth enclave of Nautilar. The war beneath the waves rages, the skaven plundering the arcane repositories of the sea aelves and abducting several Isharann in the hope of extracting the secrets of their soul-thieving magics.

THE SECOND GREAT CIVIL WAR BREWS

As the Soul Wars rage throughout the Mortal Realms, it is a time of great opportunity for the skaven. Yet true to their nature, the ratmen are so caught up in trying to keep all the spoils for themselves while slaughtering their rivals in the process that a Second Great Civil War threatens. The Clans Skryre and the Clans Pestilens vie for pre-eminence in Blight City. Everywhere skaven swarms assail the other races of the realms, seeking to steal whatever powers or technologies may give them an edge. Meanwhile, in the deepest shadows, Grey Seer Thanquol concocts fresh plans…

SKAVEN CLANS

The vast mass of skavendom consists of the five Great Clans. Each Great Clan, in turn, comprises millions of clans, each of which is an autonomous, anarchic and militarised society in its own right. The armies that these clans send forth are known as swarms, and are terrifying forces to behold.

The Great Clans – Skryre, Pestilens, Verminus, Moulder and Eshin – are immense and incredibly factionalised. Skaven legend has it that, at the very beginning of the Age of Myth, the Great Horned Rat scattered the First Clans into the darkest corners of the Mortal Realms. These were the primogenitors of each Great Clan – the first Clans Eshin, the first Clans Moulder and so forth – and there were but a handful of each. The Clans Pestilens, for example, are said to have begun as just three clans, Feesik, Septik and Morbidus, while the multitudinous Clans Verminus of the modern day supposedly originated from just two clans, Klaw and Skarrik.

The Great Horned Rat encourages constant infighting amongst his ever-multiplying broods, and from the original clans sprung dozens, then hundreds, then many thousands of splinter clans. Some faltered and failed. Many were set upon by their fellows and annihilated, reduced to slaves or re-absorbed by more powerful clans. Yet others met with success and have gone on to carve out territories of their own within the Under-Empire and to spawn their own splinter-clans.

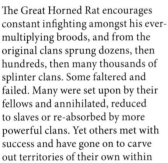

Strangely for such an anarchic and egotistical race, a clan's origins are instantly recognisable, rarely diverging far from the accepted cultural norms of their Great Clan. Every Clan Skryre, for example, emphasises arcane engineering and goes to battle armed with arrays of unstable wonder-weapons, though of course the nature of these devices varies immensely from verminous cog-automata and multi-limbed steam-driven engines to batteries of flame-hurling artillery. Each Clan Pestilens fields seething masses of Plague Monks and other diseased fanatics who make up congregations that then form the larger Virulent Processions. The Clans Verminus

rely on massed warriors and strength of numbers to fight their battles, the Clans Moulder focus on the breeding of ghastly beast-broods, and the Clans Eshin are universally devious sneak-assassins. Heraldic icons and colours very enormously from one clan to the next, and all believe themselves to be superior to their rivals, but each Great Clan retains a distinct and defined identity from one end of skavendom to the other.

'None is as much-mighty as Clawlord Vratch of Clan Gnarlkyn! So fast-fast my blade! So sharp my fangs! See-look at my many trophies, skulls of fool-things that thought they could defeat me! None will ever defeat Clawlord Vratch! I will rule Clan Gnarlkyn for a thousand years!'

- Clawlord Vratch, whose rule of Clan Gnarlkyn lasted a bloody three days

---

CLAN CONQUESTS

At its simplest, a skaven clan consists of a single leader, his viciously ambitious lieutenants and his regiments of warriors and war engines. It also includes all of the breeders, slaves and ancillary hangers-on that dig out the clan's burrows, forage its food, forge or scavenge its weapons and armour, and perform whatever menial duties are considered beneath the swaggering blade-rats that make up its armed forces. Without exception, skaven clans are geared towards conquest at all costs. Skaven always want more, be it power, territory, riches, breeders, notoriety or whatever else their fevered minds fixate upon. They are short-sighted and aggressively acquisitive, burning through resources faster than they can seize them, and the entire existence of their clans revolves around this endless race to keep pace with their own rapacity.

The clans are forever at each others' throats. Each Great Clan evidences

peculiarities of outlook and societal doctrine that actively encourage such back-biting and internecine warfare, echoes of the Horned Rat's desire for his children to scrabble ever higher in his regard up a mountain of their slain rivals. The Clans Pestilens, for example, interpret the will of the Horned Rat through unholy texts known as the Withered Word; these ever-changing scriptures emphasise the constant division and spread of the Clans Pestilens and – while the Plague Priests argue constantly about interpretations of the Withered Word and no few holy wars have been fought over them – this process of division and conquest continues apace, to the greater benefit of Pestilens as a whole.

SWARMS

Skaven armies are known as swarms, and range in size from a single leader and a clawful of regiments to a thousands-strong horde led by dozens of constantly competing skaven lords. Some hail from a single Great Clan, and may even be made up entirely of warriors from a single clan. With the differing specialisms of the Great Clans, however, it is far more common for a clan to field a swarm that incorporates supporting elements from other clans who have been hired, bribed, manipulated or blackmailed into fighting.

For example, a swarm gathered by Verminus Clan Fang might be led by a Warlord of Clan Fang and built around several Claw-hordes from that clan. It could then be supported by a number of weapon teams and warp lightning artillery pieces bartered from one of the Clans Skryre, and have scouting and assassination elements clawpledged from one of the Clans Eshin. Of course, those auxiliary elements may well have their own agendas or hidden loyalties, but those will only become clear when the double-crossing begins…

Verminlord Warbringer Thrashsnik of the Black Gnawing

Lord Hakkrit of Verminus Clan Fang

Grey Seer Skritterik

Retchtooth's Unstoppable Kill-Slayers
Claw-horde
- Clawlord Retchtooth of Verminus Clan Fang
- 1 Clawpack of Stormvermin
- 4 Clawpacks of Clanrats

Hakkrit's Forgefangs - 2 Clawpacks of Stormvermin

Vrekrit's Much-very Magnificent Killers
Claw-horde
- Clawlord Vrekrit of Verminus Clan Fang
- 3 Clawpacks of Stormvermin
- 9 Clawpacks of Clanrats

Arch-Warlock Shoktail's Smogspark Destroyers
Warpcog Convocation
- Arch-Warlock Shoktail
- 1 Arkspark Voltik Enginecoven
- 2 Gascloud Chokelung Enginecovens

(Hired in secret by Clawlord Retchtooth)

The Thirteenth Blade
Slinktalon
- Deathmaster Thwik
- 2 Clawpacks of Gutter Runners
- 4 Clawpacks of Night Runners

The Blood-Gore Grinders - 3 Doomwheels

Vrekrit's Slay-Kill Wonder-weapons
- 2 Warpfire Throwers
- 2 Clawpacks of Stormfiends
- 1 Clawpack of Jezzails

Scruntclaw's Ravenous Maw-Chewers
Fleshmeld Menagerie
- Master Moulder Scruntclaw
- Hell Pit Abomination
- 2 Clawpacks of Packmasters
- 2 Packs of Giant Rats
- 3 Packs of Rat Ogors

The Undergnaw
- 3 Warp-Grinders

The Warlock Engineers who piloted the three Doomwheels of the Blood-Gore Grinders were notoriously competitive, often racing one another into battle.

To this day, no one knows how Grey Seer Skritterik came to consume mutagen-laced warpstone and devolve into a gibbering monstrosity in the midst of the Battle for Mausol. However, it is a fact that Master Moulder Scruntclaw remains a valued – and rich – ally of Clan Fang.

Though Retchtooth believed he had hired the Thirteenth Blade as assassins, Hakkrit had paid Deathmaster Thwik substantially more to turn on his 'employer'.

Lord Hakkrit claimed his seat on the Council of Thirteen through his masterful conquest of Mausol. A towering city of bone raised by the Soulblight Vampire Zhlatomir the Unholy, Mausol had been raised atop an ancient skaven war-burrow, the defenders of which had fled the vampire's wrath and abandoned a daemon's ransom in warpstone and ancient, arcane technologies to gather dust in the darkness. The then-Clawlord Hakkrit boasted that he would hurl the Soulblight stronghold down in ruin and claim the vast wealth of Mausol for Clan Fang, and in so doing make them the most powerful of the Clans Verminus in Blight City. Hakkrit had reason for confidence, for he had the patronage of no less than a Verminlord Warbringer named Thrashnik of the Black Gnawing. This abomination had been conjured by Grey Seer Skitterik, who made a show of counselling Hakkrit, but who in truth sought to seize the riches of Mausol for the Masterclan, ideally over Hakkrit's withered corpse.

Hakkrit assembled a sizeable swarm for his assault upon Mausol, based around a huge Claw-horde led by his evil-eyed protégé Clawlord Vrekrit, and a smaller force led by the insanely paranoid Clawlord Retchtooth. He struck a deal with Arch-Warlock Shoktail of Skryre Clan Phrikk, promising the avaricious despot a portion of the lost machineries in return for his aid. He also agreed a clawpact with the revolting Master Moulder Scruntclaw of Clan Threbb, who agreed largely to spite a rival who had been courting Hakkrit's favour. The force was completed by an Eshin Slinktalon known as the Thirteenth Blade, who Retchtooth hired to shadow the swarm and strike down Clawlord Hakkrit so that Retchtooth could win favour with Grey Seer Skitterik. The machinations through which Hakkrit played his lieutenants off against one another and claimed victory are still Clan Fang legend.

THE CLANS SKRYRE

The skaven are cunning creatures, capable of great feats of ingenuity. Amongst their teeming masses there are no greater or deranged inventors than the warlocks of the Clans Skryre, who craft deadly engines of skaven supremacy for the highest bidder.

There are vast numbers of Skryre clans scattered across the Mortal Realms, varying from small bands of Warlock Engineers and their scurrying servants to massive, millions-strong hordes that inhabit sprawling fortified burrows. They gnaw out their workshop spaces inside craggy mountains or rumbling volcanoes, beneath ruined cities or through the innards of colossal ancient mechanisms that grind and churn beneath the surface of the realms.

These factory-burrows are hellish places, crammed with spinning gears, roaring furnaces, clanking pistons and copper-coil tubes that dance with caged green lightning. Unstable alchemical apparatus bubbles amongst teetering crates of machine parts and heaps of explosive munitions. The weird machines of the laboratory burrows require vast amounts of power, generated by mechanisms such as slave gangs running inside huge wooden wheels, leech-pipes sucking the vitality from slowly dying volcanoes, titanic brass batteries powered by the bubbling remains of the cursed dead, and countless other foul innovations. Barely controlled chaos reigns as construction lines churn out lethal devices at a terrifying

pace. Vast and strange are the engines of war created by these nightmarish factories, and though the Clans Skryre sell many of their contraptions to the highest bidder, they always keep the best weapons for themselves.

The sale of their surplus arsenals has made many of the Clans Skryre very rich, in turn allowing them to afford ever more excessive workshops and weapons. Some of the most successful Skryre clans possess weapons of incredible power, from the city-sized parasite engines of Clan Zikk to the giant Warp Lightning Cannons that adorn the mountainous stronghold of Clan Shokryk. Clans that have built such terrifying contraptions are feared and hated in equal measure by the rest of skavendom.

When one of the Clans Skryre sends its swarms to war, its engineers are divided into Warpcog Convocations. These formations are led by swaggering Arch-Warlocks and comprise numerous enginecovens that specialise in particular types of mechanised warfare. The Whyrlblade Threshik, for example, build great rumbling war machines covered in slicing blades that crush and hack the foe to bloody ruin. The Gautfyre Skorch, meanwhile, create hideous fire throwers, while the Arkhspark Voltik fashion batteries of lightning cannons.

While all Clans Skryre share a strong cultural link, each has its own peculiarities and pet obsessions. Even within Blight City itself there are hundreds of Clans Skryre, from the self-avowed pyromaniacs of the Clan Krakhl to the Warlock Bombardiers of Clan Shyvik who specialise in long-ranged artillery with indirect firing arcs, and the politically conniving Clan Staktik who manufacture listening devices, arcanospectral spygoggles and more for sale to the other clans of Blight City. Clan Ezzik is by far the largest

of the Clans Skryre to lurk at the heart of skavendom, and with its High Arch-Warlock Skrach sitting in the coveted first seat of the Council of Thirteen, the banner of Skryre Clan Ezzik flies above more fortress warrens and laboratory burrows by the day.

The Clans Skryre maintain plenty of strongholds beyond the bounds of Blight City. Grasping and covetous, the Clans Skryre use monstrous ether-bores and scrabbledrills to drive gnawholes into every Mortal Realm in search of technologies, warpstone and – more recently – realmstone to steal. In Aqshy, for example, the scavenge-covens of Clan Phrikk sally out from their burrows beneath the Ventruscan Hills. They pick over the ruin of others' battlefields, break into their enemies' strongholds and release billowing clouds of poisoned wind in the name of picking the dead clean of every fragment of metal and technology they can acquire. Their warrens are piled with mountains of stolen spoils, magnificent fragments of ancient artefacts heaped in with tangles of scrap in undiscerning profusion. Slave gangs pick over these huge mounds of detritus night and day, sorting the dross to be melted down for reuse and murdering one another for choice finds to bring to the warlocks in the hopes of being rewarded with their freedom.

By comparison, Clan Rhukrit – whose stronghold of Gryndfang lies beneath Ghur's Ravenous Steppes – are swift and direct. Their Whyrlblade Threshik enginecovens assemble entire spearheads of Doomwheels and Doom-Flayers that rumble across the plains in bladed convoys crushing everything in their path. Behind them come crawlburrows, mobile fortress-workshops into which go the spoils of war, and down whose ramps roll fresh waves of anarchic assault-vehicles.

*A*rch-Warlock Vrikt sat in his huge brass throne at the heart of his laboratory burrow. He was surrounded by the bedlam of heavy industry, the wails of slaves and the hiss and thunder of steam and pistons. He sneered down at the engineers prostrating themselves before him. Vrikt drummed his talons on the arms of his throne and twitched his barbed tail as he waited for the warlocks to finish fawning. His patience frayed by the moment.

'Enough!' he screeched. 'Who speaks for the Arkhspark Voltik?' After a quick bout of snarling and jostling, the lightning-engineers shoved one of their number forward. He peered up at Vrikt from behind thick-lensed goggles, doing his best to puff himself up despite his obvious terror. The engineer was actually shaking.

'I, Warlock Engineer Kratchik, talk-speak for—'

'And who for Whyrlblade Threshik?' snarled Vrikt, cutting the nervous skaven off. A burly Warlock Bombardier pushed his way to the front of his enginecoven's delegation, snapping viciously at another ratman who tried to pre-empt him.

'Warlock Bombardier Blacktail speaks, oh mighty-great Arch-Warlock,' he growled, snout jutting.

'You have-bring inventions, yes?' asked Vrikt. 'You show them now. Impress me and I will give many-much warp tokens and slaves for your workshops. Waste-fritter my time…' Vrikt left the statement hanging, and gestured with one hand-claw. The engineers' attention was drawn to a space amongst the mayhem of the laboratory, that was even now being cleared as slave gangs dragged work benches and smoke-belching mechanisms out of the way. Revealed were thirteen brass poles that jutted from the burrow floor some hundred yards distant. Lashed to each was a struggling figure, bloodied and beaten but still clad in the rags of the Gautfyre Skorch enginecoven. It brightened Vrikt's mood somewhat to see these fools offered up as test subjects. They had protested of sabotage when their fire-belcher engine blew up during a demonstration earlier that day, but their whining meant little to Vrikt. Whether incompetents or dupes, either way these failed engineers were useless to him for anything other than target practice.

The two enginecovens hurried to obey his command, pulling dirty tarpaulins off the devices they had brought. Arkhspark Voltik had created some kind of multi-barrelled lightning artillery piece, smaller than a Warp Lightning Cannon but with a fiercely destructive look to it. However, they were still busying themselves with frantic preparations when Whyrlblade Threshik hauled their own device up to the firing line. Carried by a pair of skaven, the Whyrlblade Threshik weapon consisted mainly of a huge, sprung throwing arm. Vrikt intuited that, at a trigger-pull, that arm would swing back and snatch a foot-wide circular blade from the rack lashed to the other crew-rat's back before springing forward again and hurling the blade like a huge Eshin throwing star.

'Whyrlblade Threshik offer-gifts the Rip-flinger,' announced Warlock Bombardier Blacktail. 'Ready swift-quick yes? Long-long ranged, shoots fast and kills all.' With that, the weapon's firer snapped his goggles into place, cringed slightly then pulled the trigger. The arm snapped back, grabbed a blade and flung it with tremendous force. Arch-Warlock Vrikt nodded appreciatively as the projectile sang through the air and slammed into a trussed and screeching target. The blade sliced its victim in half at the waist, with enough force left over to cut through the pole he was bound to. Metal, twitching flesh and slippery innards splattered the burrow floor.

'Again-again,' snapped Warlock Bombardier Blacktail, his muzzle twisting into an arrogant grin as the Rip-flinger snatched three more blades in quick succession and threw them. Two hit their intended target while the third span on to carome from a piston-press and mow down several luckless slaves. Impressive, thought Vrikt, and surely the victor, especially as the Arkhspark Voltik had yet to even—

The thought was cut off as there came a crackling roar and a blast of lurid green light. Vrikt was blinded and his fur stood on end. There was another blast, and another, and yet another. At last the din stopped. Blinking furiously, crouched in his throne and brandishing his warpfire projector, Vrikt sought the source of the terrifying explosions. As his sight cleared he saw that, where the Whyrlblade Threshik delegation had stood there was now naught but blackened earth and the twisted remains of charred corpses. The Rip-flinger had been reduced to smoking wreckage. Gaping, Vrikt stared at the multi-barrelled lightning cannon of Arkhspark Voltik. It was glowing as it cooled, and its crew were chittering with glee as they hurried to swap its blackened warpstone power core out for a new one. His feigned nerves now nowhere to be seen, Warlock Engineer Kratchik spat on the remains of his former rivals.

'The Rip-flinger was fast-fast, yes, but crude, and look, oh mighty Arch-Warlock, how flimsy it was! Not like the Warpraker Cannon of Arkhspark Voltik. Surely, oh great and most-mighty, there can be only one victor here.'

Vrikt sniffed, lowering himself back into his throne with as much dignity as he could muster.

'Good-good, Kratchik, most-very impressive. But there are still test-targets…'

The engineer leered his understanding and shrieked orders at his comrades. Surely, Vrikt thought with dawning paranoia, that Warlock Engineer would expect rewards and advancement. He had shown cunning, promise and ambition, entirely too much of all three. Even as the cannon fired again, the Arch-Warlock was already planning how best to send his agents into Kratchik's workshop to steal the weapon's plans and prepare an 'accident' for him. The Warpraker Cannon was magnificent, Vrikt thought, and he must have it. Its inventor, he could do without.

THE CLANS PESTILENS

The Children of the Horned Rat take many forms, the foulest of which are found within the Clans Pestilens. These zealous skaven are disciples of disease, foul harbingers of decay who hurl themselves into battle with frenzied ferocity and who seek nothing less than the final rotting of reality itself.

The Clans Pestilens form the Horned Rat's multifarious Churches of Contagion, the uncounted billions who fervently worship him in his aspect as the Great Corrupter. The ratmen of the Clans Pestilens are the most overtly religious of their race, frothing zealots who display their faith by making themselves willing hosts to the myriad diseases and parasitic malignancies of their god.

The other Great Clans seek to manipulate the denizens of the realms, or to become their tyrannical rulers. Not so the Clans Pestilens. These feculent fanatics ally or enslave the peoples of the realms when it suits their ends, but ultimately they seek dominion over a withered wasteland in which they are the only living things. The Clans Pestilens believe that the skaven will achieve this nihilistic supremacy only once their god is of one mind and one aspect – that of the Great Corruptor. The Churches of Contagion know that they must conquer not only the other races, but ultimately the other Great Clans as well. For this they require the Thirteen Great Plagues.

The Great Plagues are metaphysical diseases that strike not only at the flesh but at the soul and, in some cases, even at the warp and weft of

reality itself. Each is recorded in one of the thirteen Libers Pestilent, tomes of forbidden lore that exude spiritual foulness. To date, the Clans Pestilens have discovered eight of these terrible diseases – the eighth was seized during the latter days of the War of Life, and rumours abound of its contents and current location.

The powers of the Great Plagues have been unleashed only rarely. This is not through any sense of restraint, for such concepts are foreign to the skaven mindset. Rather, each Great Plague is a malefic concoction that requires ingredients both strange and incredibly rare and can only be brewed under specific conditions, such as the thirteenth moonrise over the red veldt or in the skull of a pox-slain arachnodon. They include such abominations as the Undulant Scourge – a tentacled parasite that bursts through the victim's flesh from a space beyond reality – the Crimsonweal Curse, which rapidly exsanguinates its victims and possesses a malign sentience that wishes only to spread to all living things, and the cannibalistic fury of the Redmaw Plague that sees its victims rend, tear and devour one another until they are dissolved by the virulent acids churning in their guts. Were the Thirteen Great Plagues to be combined in a single unholy vessel, the priest who achieved this dark miracle would bring about the Age of the Great Corruptor and the ascendancy of Pestilens.

Until that time, the Clans Pestilens continue to spread like an unstoppable plague, multiplying endlessly into ever more foetid congregations of ruin. Ancient Clans Pestilens such as Feesik, Morbidus or Septik number their Plague Monks in the billions. These are the eldest of the Clans Pestilens, claiming descent from those survivors plucked by the Great Horned Rat from the world-that-was. Within each of these

clans are hundreds of Churches of Contagion, each following slight variations upon their clan's holy writ.

Not all of the Clans Pestilens are so powerful. Countless smaller clans are forced from their warrens every year. Most often these are Churches of Contagion who have strayed into what their parent clan views as heresy. The dark gospel of the Great Corruptor – known as the Withered Word – is subjective and convoluted. Its unreliable nature owes much to the fact that many of its passages have been dictated by Plague Priests in the grip of frothing madness, or whispered from the shadows by Verminlord Corruptors whose every word drips falsehood. Combined with the skaven propensity to creatively interpret instructions, this has led to violent schisms beyond number over the centuries.

Each conflict produces further splinterings. Heretic Congregations of Filth spew like spores from their parent creed, convinced that their interpretation of the shade of buboes or the consistency of mucous is the correct one. The Withered Word dictates that such splits must happen in threes, and no Plague Priest is willing to risk the Horned Rat's displeasure by acting otherwise. Thus, when one church leaves their clan, another two will be singled out and violently ejected by rivals quick to shriek accusations of heresy for their own devious ends.

Some Clans Pestilens, such as Buborix, Corruptus and Pustulous, claim proud heritage from an ancient clan like Morbidus. Others, such as Vomikrit and Retchid, act as thrall clans to their progenitor – in this case, Feesik. Still others are so deviant that they abandon their origins altogether; the Clan Brakkish, who dwell on the flanks of the pus-volcano Expugtor in Ghyran and specialise in plague artillery, are one such wilful offshoot.

THE CLANS VERMINUS

The strength of the innumerable Clans Verminus is in their teeming swarms of Clanrats and Stormvermin. These hordes of ratmen pour across the battlefield with screeched war cries to engulf the foe in a heaving mass of lank-furred bodies and rusted blades.

It is the Clans Verminus that provide the vast quantities of warriors and slaves required to keep the armies of Blight City scurrying ever onward, and the anarchic society of the skaven thriving despite its propensity for self-destruction. The other Great Clans like to dwell upon the Verminus' lack of specialisation. They scorn the allegedly simplistic nature of Verminus' Claw-hordes

and the absence of arcane elements or lethal technologies within them. Yet the simple truth is this: without the incalculable numbers of the Clans Verminus, skavendom would eventually cease to exist.

The Clans Verminus possess strength in numbers, both in terms of the sheer size of their clans and of the myriad warriors that make up each one. Many more swarms contain at least some Verminus warriors than do not. The Grey Seers view Verminus as an inexhaustible source of ratpower, and it is a rare Arch-Warlock, Deathmaster or Master Moulder who cannot see the value of a bodyguard of burly Stormvermin or a few expendable regiments of Clanrats to fling into battle.

Far from seeing themselves as being exploited, the masters of the Clans Verminus preen and boast of their importance to skavendom; so long as it isn't their necks on the line, most Verminus warlords are more than happy to send thousands of their underlings to their deaths if it puts the members of another Great Clan in their debt.

The Clans Verminus – and particularly their heavily armed and martially minded Clawlords – are the most territorial, belligerent and aggressive of all skaven. They venerate the Great Horned Rat simply as the Conqueror, or sometimes the many-tailed King of Lashes, and they believe that he will reward those ratmen who successfully place their footclaws upon the throats of all the other sentient races in the realms.

This aggression is not reserved for external foes alone. The Clans Verminus are forever warring amongst themselves, with the pre-eminent clans rising to the top only to be cast down again in ruin. Currently, Verminus Clan Fang are the most numerous clan in all skavendom, or so they claim. Yet challengers such as the bone-armoured Clan Scour from the Realm of Light, the fiery-furred Clan Koniptik from Aqshy, the tenacious survivors of the ancient Clan Morskrit and the trophy-bedecked braggarts of Clan Vrash are already circling, watching intently for the first sign of weakness…

Clawlord Gnawdrek imperiously raised a talon to point at the beleaguered duardin battle line. 'Kill-slay!' he screeched, his order sending a scurrying tide of Clanrats surging into the enemy's guns. Gnawdrek's underlings poured across the hot desert sands beneath a hard blue-green sky, and their enemies' bullets and shells tore through them. Broken bodies and sprays of blood filled the air as the duardin fired again and again from the sandy slopes. The rippling thunder of gunfire rolled across the dunes. Gnawdrek watched impassively for a few moments before lashing his tail and drawing his hooked blade.

'Now, while the scum gnaw on their bullets, charge-charge,' snarled Gnawdrek to his Stormvermin bodyguards.

Clad in the brass and green of clan Stabbik, the hulking war-rats brandished their halberds and broke into a swift lope. Gnawdrek ran in their midst, trophy skulls rattling on his armour's back-racks. He vaulted a broken heap of Clanrats then pelted through more fallen bodies as the sand turned red beneath him.

Bullets whipped in, ricocheting from his shield or thudding into the armoured forms of his bodyguards, but though his glands tightened Gnawdrek kept going. To flee now would be to show weakness, and invite the blades of his rivals to sink into his back before darkness fell.

A cannonball roared in low, smashing the heads from three Stormvermin. Gnawdrek spat on their corpses and dug his footclaws into the thick sand. Crossing the last dozen feet between himself and the foe, the Clawlord swatted a wounded Clanrat aside then lunged and drove his blade into a beard-thing's face. Ripping his sword free, Gnawdrek bulled his way into the enemy's line. His victims were exhausted and reeling from the Clanrat onslaught, their feet tangled in mounds of skaven corpses. Gnawdrek hacked and slashed, whirling in a vicious circle to open throats and lop off limbs.

'Slaughter-kill them all!' he cried as his Stormvermin poured into the gap he had opened. 'Victory! Victory!'

THE CLANS MOULDER

The Clans Moulder are the beastmasters of the skaven race, twisters of the natural order who create monstrous abominations to loose upon the battlefield. Their rapacious war beasts are greatly feared across the Mortal Realms. Even amongst their cruel race, the Clans Moulder have a dark reputation.

The Master Moulders of the Clans Moulder use weird alchemy, crude surgery and blasphemous dark magic to meld disparate creatures together and create terrible aberrations. From vast albino monstrosities that rend tunnels through the bedrock of the realms, to seething tides of flea-infested fiends that devour everything in their path, the Clans Moulder are responsible for the creation of some of the most hideous terrors employed by any race in war. Amongst these are certain favoured breeds of war beast – Rat Ogors and Giant Rats chief amongst them – that have secured the position of the Clans Moulder as a real power in skavendom. The secrets behind the creation of such abhorrent flesh hulks as the Hell Pit Abominations, meanwhile, are amongst the most valuable that the Clans Moulder possess. Countless spies from other clans have been used as brood fodder for daring to try to steal them.

The Clans Moulder worship the Great Horned Rat in his aspect as the Writhing Broodsire, a protean nightmare of ever-multiplying verminous flesh whose fecundity they wish to bring into reality so that it buries all the realms. The Clans' Packmasters are renowned as surly and crude individuals, more akin to the brutish beasts they herd than the rest of their cunning race, and their disgusting belief system doesn't help matters. Moreover, many members of the Clans Moulder are tainted and twisted by the warpstone-based procedures they use to create their war beasts – they may be bloated and hairless, have glowing eyes, be always voraciously hungry, or possess additional tails or limbs.

Currently, the most powerful of all the Clans Moulder is Clan Dregg, whose Master Moulder Zhurn Aelf-eater holds the tenth seat on the Council of Thirteen. Dregg are renowned for the sheer fecund numbers of their beasts, and hold lucrative contracts with many Clans Verminus and Skryre. However, they are far from the only major power amongst the Clans Moulder.

In Ghyran, for example, the Clan Threbb channel perverted life magics into their war beasts in order to keep them regenerating far past all sane notions of resilience. The sinister skin-and-bone creations of Shyishan Clan Snirk are terrible to behold, while all have cause to fear the grotesquely modified snatch-packs of Clan Ghrubbitus, who spirit away enemy champions and leaders – skaven or otherwise – to serve as unwilling subjects for experimentation and high-level breeding programs.

*A*t first glance, the revivification pit looked to be full of mangled remains. Mounds of flesh and scabrous clumps of fur were piled high amongst drifts of wet muscle, jutting fangs and claws, blinded eyes and other, less easily identifiable organic detritus.

Master Moulder Sturknik saw past the revolting anarchy. As he stared down into the massive pit, his practised gaze picked out the stitches that bound fleshy sacs and bloated limbs together. He saw the gland-clusters where they had been melded with warp-engines and viscid tangles of exposed nerves. In his mind's eye, the corpulent skaven saw the beast as it would soon look, rather than this obscene jumble of parts.

'It awaits only the spark-touch of the Writhing Broodsire,' he hissed through his crooked fangs, and his attendant Packmasters nodded and muttered in agreement. 'It lurks beyond the veil,' cried Sturknik, his eyes bulging with mad intensity. 'We must goad-goad it forth! Throw the first lever!'

Three of his underlings dashed to obey, the largest kicking and clawing the other two away from the huge brass lever. He wrapped both hand-claws and his tail around the control and gave it a mighty wrench. The lever fell with a loud thunk, and warp lightning coursed down the extended wakening vanes. Energies arced, leaping into the pit and crawling across the huge carcass curled there. Sturknik felt triumph rise in his chest as it twitched and jerked.

'The second lever! The third! Pull-throw them all!' he screeched, and his Packmasters did so with gusto. Blast after blast, bolt after bolt of lurid green energy stabbed down into the monster's body. The stench of cooking flesh filled the air. Smoke rose, and suddenly Sturknik felt a subsonic growl shudder through his bones.

Amidst a last cannonade of lightning blasts, the Hell Pit Abomination unfolded itself like a vast and verminous worm and reared up to roar with myriad gaping maws. The beast was alive, and it was hungry…

THE CLANS ESHIN

The most shadowy and mysterious of all the skaven, the Clans Eshin are versed in the arts of stealth and assassination, poison and spycraft. They are seen as hired killers and slinking back-stabbers. Yet there is much more to the Clans Eshin and their hidden agenda than mere mercenary assassins.

Not even the Masterclan know very much about the hidden enclaves and secretive practices of the Clans Eshin. Where they hide their shadowy, heavily fortified burrows is a secret that many have died to protect. How the Clans Eshin train their deadly killers or instil in them a discipline so utterly lacking in most skaven is also a mystery. Who are the mysterious Masters that rule their clans and disguise their identities through illusion, body-doubles and webs of misdirection? What are the Clans Eshin's true goals? Why, when they have such lethal agents of assassination at their disposal, have they never made a bid for control of Blight City? These are question that play upon the minds of all skaven who have dealings with the Clans Eshin, filling them with paranoia and outright fear.

In truth, this aura of ominous mystery is just another weapon in the arsenal of the Clans Eshin. And they have many, many weapons. Supernaturally fast and possessed of incredible agility, their agents are well versed in the arts of unarmed combat, bladesmanship, explosives, poisons, firearms, throwing weapons, and any other method of delivering a swift kill that their elusive Masters believe may give them an edge. The most accomplished agents of the Clans Eshin can walk on shadow, and slip through holes no larger than a coin. These sinister skaven evade the staunchest guards and most potent magical wards to leave their victims mysteriously slain, or else vanished altogether, never to be seen again.

This is not to say that the strength of the Clans Eshin lies only in small-scale missions of assassination and intrigue. When they choose to move in force, packs of Night Runners and Gutter Runners attack in their hundreds, using stealth, blurring speed and feral cunning to surround and overwhelm their enemies. The foe's advance guards are ambushed and buried in furry bodies that stab and bite frantically before disappearing to leave only corpses in their wake. Artillery crews and other rear-echelon assets are annihilated by skaven striking from unexpected quarters. Enemy officers are hit from all sides by hurtling throwing stars and envenomed daggers before the skaven assassins leap from the shadows to finish off their weakened quarry. Then come the terrifying Verminlord Deceivers, slipping from the dark spaces behind reality to strike the heads from the enemy's commanders and send the last of their warriors fleeing in mindless terror.

The Clans Eshin see the Great Horned Rat as the Shadow of Murder, a secretive abomination that compels them to slay all those who hold positions of power, and to spread anarchy, confusion and panic among their rivals until they – and they alone – possess the information and wherewithal to rule. All of their hit-and-run battles and elaborate covert missions are executed with this goal in mind and, though they would never reveal as much to the other Great Clans, Eshin seek to destabilise their fellow skaven as much as they do the other sentient races of the Mortal Realms.

The greatest strength of the Clans Eshin is believed to lie hidden in the dark corners of Ulgu, the Realm of Shadow. How many fortress-warrens they maintain there, how they are hidden and what strength of warriors they contain are questions to which the Masterclan are forever seeking answers. Few are forthcoming. Indeed, even the names and markings of the Clans Eshin are typically kept vague and mysterious.

Clan Scurrie and Clan Stryk give the appearance of being the two largest and most powerful of these shadowy clans, for both possess strong presences in Blight City, and both have a Master seated upon the Council of Thirteen. It is known that Scurrie specialise in assassination through the use of complex gadgetry such as gnawbombs, warp-grinders and telescoping blades – they are believed to maintain strong ties with at least one of the Clans Skryre – and that their agents can be recognised by the distinctive clan rune branded into their flesh or stained upon their fur. Clan Stryk, by comparison, are believed to be masters of subtle poisons and contact-venoms, achieving many of their kills without ever seeming to raise a claw in anger. Their agents are believed to wear garb of black and dark purple, and communicate in a secret tongue that even the Masterclan have never been able to decipher.

Of course, what is believed about the Clans Eshin and what is the truth can be two wholly different things; it is possible that Scurrie and Stryk are far from the most powerful clans amongst the Eshin ranks, that they are but false fronts or even that they are not who they say they are at all. Meanwhile, even less is known about clans such as black-furred Clan Nichtus, the expert saboteurs of Clan Kratt or the grey-cowled mage-slayers of Clan Nullix. Most know only that the Clans Eshin are to be feared…

THE MASTERCLAN

Even amongst a race as devious and self-serving as the skaven, there are those with minds so cunning that they are able to manipulate the rest of their species into doing their bidding. Such is the nature of the Masterclan, whose seers and daemons direct the swarms of skavendom on the road to ultimate victory.

Through sorcerous might, force of arms and a dizzying array of trickery, back-stabbing, bribery and deceit is the skaven race ruled. The Council of Thirteen believe themselves to be the absolute masters of the Under-Empire and – to some degree – they are correct. Yet in truth, at least as often as they enact their own wills, the Lords of Decay are actually serving the ends of the Masterclan whether purposefully or through being subtly manipulated.

The Masterclan is far smaller than any of the Great Clans, its numbers minuscule by comparison. Indeed, there are mere clans in skavendom whose numbers are greater than all the Grey Seers of the Masterclan combined. Yet even the least Grey Seer is a powerful practitioner of dark sorcery, their skulls crowned by curling horns, their minds ever churning with a million underhand schemes and devious thoughts. Like parasites lodged in the brain of an infinitely larger beast, the Grey Seers compel the vast mass of their species to follow their commands, while using the might and numbers of the Great Clans to bolster their own power.

There are representatives of the Masterclan on the Council of Thirteen, and if questioned, the other Lords of Decay would all claim that their own influence equals – if not exceeds – that of the grey-furred sorcerers. This is how the order of Grey Seers prefers to keep it, for they have found the Great Clans more biddable if their arrogant leaders believe the Grey Seers to be at their beck and call rather than the other way around. Yet the truth is that – even as they give the impression of enacting the will of the council – the Masterclan is nearly always three clawsteps ahead. They must be, for they are the prophets of the Horned Rat as a single, unified deity, and it is their duty to interpret and enact his will no matter the cost (to any but themselves, of course!).

Grey Seers spend much of their time operating behind the scenes in the Under-Empire. They emerge from their heavily guarded warrens only when accompanied by a bodyguard of hulking albino Stormvermin whose loyalty to their masters has been sorcerously or alchemically ensured. The rest of their time is spent plotting and scheming, scrying faraway developments and manoeuvring their rivals with deft claw-twitches and cunning ploys.

Nor are the Grey Seers immune to the lure of politicking and the pursuit of power. Orders can be misinterpreted, after all, or misunderstood by dullard underlings who – through no fault of the Grey Seer's, they would protest – end up perpetrating massacres or enacting retreats that coincidentally further the seers' agendas. The rivalries between the Grey Seers are legendary, and the power games these supposed leaders engage in with one another can see invasions derailed and clans exterminated wholesale.

For all this, when they do take to the field of battle, the Grey Seers are to be feared. They possess a ferocious grasp of the arcane arts, wielding horrific magics that can summon tides of ravenous vermin, or rip open the lands so that noxious fumes and scorching flame consume their enemies. They can even call forth unnatural tempests from the beyond to ground airborne enemies, and should they find themselves in imminent danger, they are able to teleport across the battlefield in great 'skitterleaps'. Yet it is the Grey Seers' frenzied intellect that is perhaps their most deadly weapon of all. They are arch-manipulators possessed of a rabid desire to control all that they survey, and when they turn their wits to military victory it takes a truly great mind to match their puissance and willingness to sacrifice their own warriors in the name of victory.

When compelled to go to war in person, many Grey Seers ride high upon the creaking carriages of Screaming Bells. Of all the diabolical wonder-weapons of the skaven, none is more iconic nor more dreaded by their enemies. They take the form of massive brazen bells, swinging within an arched carriage of stone, metal and wood and heaved into battle by frenzied masses of wild-eyed ratmen, and their dolorous peals have been harbingers of doom for countless civilisations across the Mortal Realms.

The bell is an ever-present symbol in the mythology of the skaven, and the mighty toll of each Screaming Bell strikes deep inside the black hearts of the ratmen. They inspire awe, fear, and the closest thing to devotion the skaven can achieve. From atop these unholy altars the Grey Seers preach their plans of total domination in the name of the Great Horned Rat.

Each Screaming Bell is an unholy relic, cast in the hellish warpforges beneath Blight City using brass laced with pure warpstone. Warlock Engineers from Clan Resnykt – who have grown rich off the secrets of creating these potent artefacts – and Grey Seers engage in a thirteen-day ritual to create each bell. Their chittering incantations cause glowing balefire runes to writhe mystically across the surface of the bell, and as the casting is cooled, the metal is coated many times with sacrificial blood. The result is a magical terror-weapon whose peals roll out across the battlefield in waves of physical force. Each thunderclap of sound sends enemies reeling in terror and pain, even as it reverberates a message of inevitable skaven supremacy that sends the ratmen surging into battle with froth spilling from their jaws. Stone shatters, the enemy's bones are pulverised to dust and – as the peals grow ever louder – even reality itself is split asunder by the unnatural cacophony of the Screaming Bell.

THANQUOL AND BONERIPPER

Rabidly ambitious, as inspired as he is delusional, and dangerously addicted to devouring warpstone, Grey Seer Thanquol is a loose cannon. He inspires a mix of envy and hatred amongst his peers, for his schemes are so entangled as to bewilder even the other Grey Seers – at least until they come to improbable spectacular fruition or else blow up in his face. If there is one thing Thanquol possesses in abundance, it is self-confidence; so convinced is he of his own genius that he can swiftly shift any blame for failure to the first available victim, adapt his plans to account for – or even capitalise on – catastrophe, and simply press on.

Traditionally, Thanquol has been accompanied by a monstrous Rat Ogor called Boneripper. The first of these beasts was slain long ago, serving as a fleshy bulwark for its shrieking master. However, Thanquol is surprisingly sentimental about this brute, and after each loss has always commissioned agents of the Clans Skryre and Moulder to fashion him a new and usually improved beast to serve as bodyguard and steed.

Rumour has it that Thanquol is ancient, that the Horned Rat plucked him from the world-that-was and imprisoned him for some grandiose error, and that he gnawed his way free. Certainly he has appeared suddenly in Blight City, playing many sides against the middle in a frenetic bid to accumulate power. Does Thanquol seek a seat on the Council of Thirteen? Is he under the Horned Rat's protection, or is he on the run from his god and blessed with obscene good fortune? Skavendom seethes with questions about this shadowy figure…

Grey Seer Thanquol crouches atop the broad shoulders of his monstrous Rat Ogor, Boneripper. The beast's censer-fists billow poisonous warpstone fumes as its master screeches the jagged words to an arcane invocation.

VERMINLORDS

To behold a Verminlord is to see a splinter of the Great Horned Rat himself. It is to see creeping decay and inscrutable knowledge made manifest, anarchic ambition and insidious malice given physical form. These towering rat daemons are living icons of ruin, the ultimate scavengers from beyond the veil.

Verminlords are exemplars of everything a skaven aspires to be. Insanely cunning, malevolent and menacing, viciously strong, whip-fast and eternally manipulative, they are the daemons of the Horned Rat. Verminlords loom above the hierarchy of skaven society. They see all other Verminlords as rivals and all mortal skaven as pawns in their ongoing schemes. However, the Grey Seers of the Masterclan cling to the boast that the Verminlords are theirs to summon and to bargain with as they see fit, and that they are thus tools of the Masterclan rather than the other way around.

It suits the Verminlords to permit this charade; even the daemons of the Horned Rat like to have an incompetent minion or two to blame should matters go awry, and it befits the Verminlords' sinister natures to manipulate from the shadows wherever they can. It is for this reason that certain rat daemons act as patrons for particularly promising skaven leaders; they whisper advice into their twitching ears and ensure horrible fates befall their rivals.

However, for all their dark bargains and politicking, when a Verminlord steps into the light and flexes its monstrous talons, there can be no doubt who is the master and who the slave.

Just as the Horned Rat is split into different aspects, so his Verminlords reflect these personas. They are divided into the Warbringers, Deceivers, Corruptors, Warpseers and other rarer and stranger castes. Certain of these beings are drawn to particular Great Clans whose aspects echo their own, and are held up by those clans' leaders as vengeful totems. Verminlords manipulate and terrify any and all skaven into doing their bidding – it is simply that they are most likely to manifest alongside those ratmen whose methods are most pleasing to them.

Verminlord Warbringers are the most commonly seen of the rat daemons, especially amongst the Clans Verminus, and of all the Verminlords they are the most arrogant, aggressive and territorial. Warbringers have a fondness for

dramatic entrances, arriving in clouds of smoke before mustered skaven hordes, or tearing their way into reality through the screaming form of an enemy champion. Their egotism and showmanship are not baseless, however, for few foes can match the speed and strength of a Verminlord Warbringer when its blood is up. Meanwhile, their presence spreads a supernatural fervour through their underlings.

Verminlord Deceivers, by comparison, are subtle and secretive killers whose daemonic might is complemented by supernatural stealth and skill. Closely associated with the Clans Eshin, these half-seen terrors move amidst clouds of obfuscating shadow and speak in ominous whispers, their every utterance echoing thirteen times over in a chorus of subtly differing lies. When they strike, they burst forth with blistering speed to slide their warpstilettos through their victims' ribs, or fling their spinning doomstars to lop off heads before the fiendish weapons return to their waiting talons.

SKREECH VERMINKING

Dark tales tell of a Verminlord like no other, a terror by the name of Skreech Verminking. It is said this fell being began as an entire Council of Thirteen, twelve Lords of Decay snatched up by the Great Horned Rat and cast into a shadowed oubliette. These were the most devious, the most wicked and malevolent council there has ever been. Their plots wound about one another like twining rats' tails, and their efforts to undermine one another saw them scale new heights of cunning and conquest. Then came a scheme unlike any other, all twelve Lords of Decay clawpledging to work as one until their great undertaking was complete. Little could they know that their god heard them make this vow, and the hideous fate it would lead them to. Some versions of the legend claim the council sought to gnaw away the void around the Realm of Heavens and send it crashing down in ruin. Others tell how the council pursued the secret of immortality. Some even whisper that they were fashioning a weapon that could kill gods, and that the Horned Rat suspected his children of attempting

to slay and supplant him as they would one another. Whatever the truth, their punishment was hideous. Millennia trapped in a metaphysical prison, their only nourishment the tattered remnants of failed schemes, their only pastime an endless round of recrimination and talon-pointing. When at last the Horned Rat relented and plucked the Lords of Decay from their prison, what emerged was not twelve individual beings but a hideous amalgamation of them all. Twisted and tail-locked, they were now one squirming abomination that mutated further in the Horned One's grip until at last it arose as the mightiest Verminlord of all time. So Skreech Verminking came into being. He possessed every scrap of knowledge ever accumulated by the skaven race, and the absolute desire to see the Horned Rat reign supreme. Since that day, Skreech Verminking has led the Shadow Council in its machinations, unleashed terrible curses and monstrous fates upon countless civilisations, and commanded skaven swarms in battles that have brought entire races to ruin. He is the left claw of the Horned Rat, and he is doom to all who look upon him.

Verminlord Corruptors are demigods of the Clans Pestilens. They are the daemonic avatars of the Great Corruptor, fonts of eldritch ruination. Foulness runs through their clotted veins, lice teem in their scabrous pelts, and their flesh reeks of decay. Verminlord Corruptors are fanatics, single-minded in the spreading of disease and entropy. They wield plaguereapers with savage skill even as they vomit geysers of rancid filth and chitter dark prayers that unleash noxious blights upon any unlucky enough to be stood nearby.

Verminlord Warpseers are the most inscrutable of their kind. They are manipulators and schemers who manifest to take command of skaven swarms wherever it will further their labyrinthine plots. Their strength lies in the arcane arts above all else; these rat daemons are able to conjure forth dark lightnings and unleash withering curses upon their enemies with every hissed syllable. The paths of the future are also theirs to see, for the Warpseers can summon pulsating scry-orbs that reveal to them all the secrets they wish to know. In extremis, these orbs can be flung as a weapon, detonating in a cascade of fractured futures and splintered possibilities that drives the foe to madness and despair.

A Verminlord Warbringer strikes a conqueror's pose, taunting his enemies with his martial might even as he prepares to butcher them for the glory of the Horned Rat.

WARLOCKS AND WEAPONS OF SKRYRE

The Clans Skryre fight their battles using a mixture of dark sorcery and arcane engineering. The warlocks that lead their covens go to battle festooned with bizarre contraptions for the channelling of magical energies, and their potent wonder-weapons can blast gaping holes in the enemy battle line with every shot.

SKRYRE WARLOCKS

The warlocks of the Clans Skryre are the artificers of skaven society. They blend arcane sorceries with technology in an insane and mind-boggling mix, using strange contraptions like warp-power accumulators and thaumognaw-accelerators to channel the magic of the realms into blasts of dark lightning.

The greatest amongst their number – those warlocks who have successfully risen to control their clans through politicking, assassination and shows of force – are known as Arch-Warlocks. While smaller Clans Skryre or expeditionary swarms may be led by just one of these eldritch beings, many clans are led by entire mastercovens of them. Clad in elaborate suits of warpstone-powered armour, these potent engineer-warriors can unleash blasts of sorcerous energy and roiling tongues of warpflame from high-tech projectors while their interlocking brass plates protect them from harm.

There are many different schools of engineering scattered throughout the Clans Skryre, with individual warlocks choosing whatever specialism they believe will best allow them to realise their megalomaniacal ambitions while putting paid to their rivals in violent and explosive fashion. Many become Warlock Engineers, whose areas of construction and sorcery are broad and varied. Skilled in the creation of weapons of war and the conjuring of warp lightning through techno-sorcerous devices, Warlock Engineers prefer to put paid to their enemies at a distance. When cornered and forced to fight, however, their crackling warp-energy blades and potent warplock pistols can make a bloody mess of even the toughest foes.

Other warlocks become slowly more obsessed with particular areas of arcane death-dealing, from the gas-jetting Warlock Fumigators to the esoteric sciences of the Warlock Shattertalons who guide the drill-engines used to fashion gnawholes.

Warlock Bombardiers, meanwhile become ever more fixated on wreaking destruction with explosives launched from afar. Alongside their ability to channel and unleash warp lightning, These skaven specialise in long-ranged ballistic devastation. Their favoured weapons are the doomrockets that they build in their precarious workshops.

A doomrocket consists of a long brass pole fitted with a trigger and warp-volt sparking mechanisms, upon which is a affixed a sizeable warhead. When the Warlock Bombardier points his rocket in the general direction of the foe and squeezes the trigger, a shock of warp lightning runs up the insulated pole and sparks off the propellant in the doomrocket's base. There comes a fiery roar as the doomrocket leaps from its launcher and races through the air, slamming into the ground in the enemy's midst to detonate with a ferocious boom and blinding green flash. When the smoke clears, hideous devastation is revealed in the explosion's wake.

Different Warlock Bombardiers prefer to fashion alternative types of warheads for their weapon, often dictated by their enginecoven allegiance. Thus, those Bombardiers belonging to Whyrlblade Threshik tend towards flechette bombs, while Gascloud Chokelung Bombardiers create long-range poisoned wind bombs, and those of the Gautfyre Skorch fashion warheads that explode in sprays of corrosive warpfire.

SKRYRE ACOLYTES

While the warlocks form their covens to rule over the Clans Skryre, the great mass of ratmen below them are known as Acolytes. These skaven scurry in their masters' shadows. They fetch, carry, tinker, aid with experimentation and bully slave gangs into running in their wheels or 'volunteering' to test the warlocks' weapons.

Every Acolyte has a singular desire – to rise to the rank of warlock either through the favour of his betters or by murdering one of them and claiming their workshop for his own. In the meantime, the Acolytes fight for their clan by donning heavy gas-hoods, robes and goggles, shouldering gasp-breather backpacks and taking to the field armed with bandoliers of volatile poisoned wind globes. These fragile spheres of glass are filled with toxic warpstone-derived fumes produced by the warlocks in their laboratories and named poisoned wind.

Poisoned wind globes are much feared by the skaven's enemies, for armour is no defence against the seeping gas they release upon shattering, and even thick cloth hoods and rubberised seals quickly break down beneath the corrosive fume. Those who breathe poisoned wind find their lungs filling with fluid, their flesh breaking out in agonising blisters and their eyes dissolving and weeping from their sockets. Death comes soon after, an agonising dissolution as the victim is eaten away from without and within. Acolytes hurl volley after volley of poisoned wind globes into the enemy's ranks and – barring catastrophic mishaps with the fragile and easily dropped spheres – can rapidly annihilate even the most resilient foes.

DOOMWHEELS

Few devices sum up the crazed ingenuity of the skaven better than the infernal war engine known as the Doomwheel. At first, the Doomwheel might seem ludicrous to those who have never seen one in battle. This delusion is soon shattered as the war engine ploughs into the enemy lines, spitting bolts of coruscating warp lightning while crushing everything in its path to bloody paste.

Rats scampering on twin treadmills inside an enormous wheel provide the primary motive force of this bizarre machine. This, in turn, sparks the warpstone generator that – if all goes well – discharges bolts of lethal warp lightning. If the green-black bolts that arc out from the warp conduits do not slay the foe, then it will be up to the great iron-banded wheel to crush all who dare to stand in the Doomwheel's path. At the centre of the contraption sits a Warlock Engineer pilot. Occupying this mighty work of death-dealing artifice leaves the warlock so full of bold reassurance that the otherwise dubious courage of his race is, at least partially, offset. Doubtless, the wafting fumes from the warpstone generator bolster the engineer's confidence as well.

Of course, there are always 'technical challenges' that make the Doomwheel dangerously haphazard. For instance, the rat propulsion system of the Doomwheel might, on occasion, produce results that veer between mildly disappointing and deeply lethargic. At the same time, it is not uncommon for an overstressed warpstone generator to fire arcs of lightning at random, or to simply detonate in spectacular fashion. The Warlock Engineer who pilots the Doomwheel also has much to attend to – ensuring that the warpstone generator is not overloading, or goading the rats of the propulsion system with a shock-prod. Sometimes, steering is a duty that must be temporarily abandoned due to more immediate concerns, and it is not uncommon to see Doomwheels plough through a pack or two of allies before they slam into the enemy lines. Random, cruel and undeserved death is nothing new for the skaven, however, and so long as Doomwheels continue to rip through the foe's formations with such breathtaking effectiveness, they will continue to be built.

WEAPON TEAMS

The Clans Skryre churn out mountains of materiel every day, more weapons of war than they could ever possibly wield by themselves. A great many of these are cumbersome weapons of destruction intended to be borne by a pair of skaven known as a weapon team. Whether carried into battle by dedicated Skryre Acolytes or sold to the other Great Clans to be crewed by whichever overconfident fools can be talked into the job, these wonder-weapons can wreak horrible devastation amongst the enemy – at least until their inevitable, often spectacular malfunction.

For ranged mass carnage, the Warpfire Thrower and the Ratling Gun are both extremely popular weapons – at least with those skaven not standing too close when they're fired. The former pipes a warpstone-infused alchemical solution from a sloshing tank into a heavy nozzle, through which it is sprayed in gouts across the enemy. The viscous mix ignites on contact with the air, bursting into ferocious green-black flames that scorch their victims to the bone while the crew-rats squeal with savage glee. Ratling Guns, meanwhile, are multi-barrelled whirling death-machines. Powered by warp-steam and kicked into gear by the frenzied working of a hand-crank, the six barrels of the Ratling Gun spin and whir, spitting a fusillade of warpstone-laced bullets that tear rank after rank of the foe to bloody shreds. Overheating can lead to an explosive misfire – always a danger once the skaven crew begin maniacally cranking and firing for all they are worth – but the carnage they cause first more than makes up for this dubious instability.

The Doom-Flayer is a truly unsubtle tool of slaughter. This motorised metal ball of whirling blades was originally developed for tunnel clearance in subterranean warfare. A warpstone generator powers the contraption, with one lurking skaven tending its temperamental motor and keeping the Doom-Flayer moving. The other crew-rat steers, shrieking and cackling maniacally as his vehicle ploughs through the enemy ranks amidst sprays of gore and spills of viscera. Of course, should the Doom-Flayer stall in the midst of the foe, their vengeance is often swift and bloody.

Strangest of all the commonly seen weapon teams is the Warp-Grinder. Originally intended as a device to help the skaven tunnel more quickly, this weapon's warp-energy projector pulverises compacted earth, rock and even metal in a wide area, leaving a narrow, smoking tunnel in its wake. Though cave-ins and meltdowns of the weapon are a constant danger, groups of skaven can scurry along the tunnel in the Warp-Grinder's wake and – with some margin for user-error – burst up from the ground to fall upon the enemy's undefended flank or rear. The Warp-Grinder is especially popular with the Clans Eshin, who use it to slip bands of Gutter Runners into the enemy's midst. It doesn't hurt that the Warp-Grinder itself, while not primarily designed for combat, can pulverise enemy warriors and war engines as easily as it does bedrock.

WARP LIGHTNING CANNONS

The Warp Lightning Cannon is a contraption built by the fiendishly clever Warlock Engineers of the Arkhspark Voltik enginecovens, and is powered by an enormous hunk of warpstone. This war machine generates an unearthly charge with massive destructive potential, which is directed along a rune-etched barrel forged and enchanted to channel its fury.

When fired, the Warp Lightning Cannon emits a sizzling ball of warp energy. Any skaven near the weapon at the time get a shock, causing their fur to stand on end and searing sickly green after-images across their vision. The bolt arcs groundwards, punching through anything in its path and then erupting in a crackling storm of warp lightning. The shot travels too quickly to follow, but its trail is easily marked. Blackened corpses twitch in its wake, and anything large enough to fully interpose itself between the bolt and its target is left with a smouldering hole several feet wide punched through it. Naturally, Warp Lightning Cannons make excellent siege weapons, for rare are the gates or walls that can long absorb the punishment these weapons can mete out – at least so long as the crew-rats do not overload their weapon and blow themselves to smithereens.

STORMFIENDS

Rat Ogors are hulking beasts stitched together out of component parts harvested or grown by the Clans Moulder. Purchased in a still-gestative state from the moulders by the Clans Skryre, these mindlessly violent war beasts are biologically boosted with warpstone serums and augmented with arcane technologies to become something truly abominable.

Larger still than a normal Rat Ogor and boasting skin-fused armour plates, Stormfiends are amongst the most terrifying weapons to emerge from Blight City. Furthermore, Stormfiends overcome the greatest weakness suffered by unaugmented Rat Ogors – that of a very small

brain. This is achieved by the gruesome expedient of suturing atrophied 'brain-skaven' directly to their backs. These vile beings are fused to their monstrous charges with wires and tubes, their own bodies withering until they become little more than auxiliary minds whose only purpose is to guide the Stormfiends and direct their fury.

As if their phenomenal resilience, virtual immunity to pain and shield-crushing strength were not enough, the Clans Skryre further arm Stormfiends with an arsenal of spectacularly destructive weaponry. This transforms them into either walking artillery pieces or line-breaking assault units with few equals. Moreover, directed by their vestigial brain-rats, they stomp forwards with beady-eyed determination, holding to their simple but destructive purpose no matter the odds against them.

Stormfiends armed with ratling cannons can lay down screaming hails of hot warp-lead bullets that reduce swathes of the enemy to red mist in moments. Those with warpfire projectors shoot torrents of green-black flame over great distances that dissolve anything they come into contact with, while those armed with windlaunchers hurl poisoned wind grenades into the foe's midst, where the corrosive gases they release swiftly render flesh and metal alike into bubbling goo.

By comparison, Stormfiends with doomflayer gauntlets annihilate their enemies in hand-to-hand combat with huge motorised iron balls and arrays of whirring blades.

Those bearing shock gauntlets are transformed into walking lightning-generators, lethal energies arcing off them in all directions to annihilate anyone luckless enough to be stood nearby. Then there are the grinderfists, which combine the ability to tunnel through the bedrock of the battlefield and attack from unexpected quarters with the capacity to churn through armour, flesh and bone with hideous efficiency.

WARPLOCK JEZZAILS

Warplock Jezzails are long-barrelled rifles that require a two-skaven team to load and fire, and loose high-velocity rounds made of refined warpstone that strike with enough force to punch through even sigmarite plate. The glowing warp-bullets leave vivid green trails as they rip through the air, and impact with a deafening and highly distinctive crack. Victims struck by jezzail fire are smashed off their feet as though hit by a wrecking ball.

Jezzails are popular weapons within skavendom amongst hired killers, for they allow their wielder to strike quickly, from a great distance and without their target knowing the danger until it is too late. Of course, not every target has the good grace to die from a single shot – protective warding, inhuman resilience, inconvenient crosswinds or simple inaccuracy by the highly strung skaven marksmen can lead to the jezzail teams coming under attack from their erstwhile victims. To this end, each jezzail is equipped with a bulky pavise designed to protect the weapon's operators from return fire.

Lightweight in comparison to the equipment carried by other weapon teams, quick to relocate and easy to maintain, Warplock Jezzails are favoured by the Clans Eshin, and by those Skryre forces making war amidst ruined forts and settlements. Many an enemy hero has been felled by a sudden volley from a leaning spire or crumbling belfry, and when deployed atop commanding vantage points, these weapons can turn entire regions of any battlefield into lethal no-go zones for the foe.

THE FLESHSCORCHERS

Skryre Clan Krakhl are amongst the most prolific wielders of warpfire as a weapon in battle. Their lurid green livery is forever singed at the edges, their fur burned away in blackened patches and their flesh stained with soot and ash. Many skaven of this clan are badly disfigured by warpfire burns, some even showing bare bone through their ravaged flesh. Yet nothing stays their pyromania. Infamous amongst the ranks of Clan Krakhl are the Fleshscorchers, a sub-cult of engineers driven to bear warpfire throwers into battle and there douse their enemies in glowing flame. Most Warlock Engineers wouldn't risk standing within thirteen paces of an active warpfire thrower, yet the Fleshscorchers tinker constantly with their unstable gear to maximise its output – even in the heat of battle – and insist on unleashing their weapons' fury in person. Such is his arrogance that each engineer believes himself too skilled to fall foul of mechanical malfunction, and each is sure that he will be the one to build and unleash the ultimate warpfire thrower.

DEVOTEES OF PESTILENS

The Clans Pestilens are the most overtly religious of all the Children of the Horned Rat. They are deranged zealots whose swarms rely upon numbers and ferocity, coupled with the deleterious effects of their weaponised plagues, to rapidly wear their enemies down before a last headlong charge sees them annihilated wholesale.

PLAGUE PRIESTS

Plague Priests are the fanatical leaders of the Churches of Contagion. Entire conclaves of these rancid beings rule over each of the Clans Pestilens, maintaining their tenuous grip on power through zealotry, cunning and outright violence. They wield warpstone-tipped staves that rot all they touch, or foul plague censers that belch clouds of diseased smog across the enemy, and can spit forth the words of pestilent prayers that reduce the foe to plague-riddled corpses in moments.

The Plague Priests of the Horned Rat are frothing lunatics, ranting preachers of the Withered Word and true believers in the Great Corruptor. These diseased fanatics are unusual in skaven terms for their propensity to lead from the front. They hack, claw and bite their way through their enemies while screeching prayers that conjure unholy miracles or blessings of foetid filth. Some Plague Priests fight in this seemingly courageous fashion because their sanity is so eroded that they do not recognise their own danger. Most simply seek to win the Horned Rat's favour, and will gladly use their underlings as living shields at the first sign of real peril.

To the Plague Priests, winning their verminous god's blessing is their main goal, for it is vital in their climb towards ever greater power. Even the smallest Clans Pestilens are led by several competing Plague Priests. The largest have hundreds, even thousands of these vile beings to drive their swarms into battle, and to lead the devoted chitterings of their congregations in praise of the Great Corruptor. The internal hierarchies of these priesthoods are convoluted in the extreme, but all hinge around violence and fear.

The Plague Priests within any given clan vie constantly for dominance, and will resort to any act of bribery, coercion or back-stabbing to rise above their rivals. A common tactic employed by the priests of Pestilens is inventing new and ever-more-important-sounding titles for themselves. These names are tied to the priests' duties within the church, and are ridiculously overblown; names such as the Most-blessed Master of the Chittering Chant or the Arch-Squealer of the Followers of the Furnace impress dull minds – reason enough to tear the throat out of anyone foolish enough to laugh at them.

All Plague Priests have at least some ability in brewing the plagues and toxic concoctions that their clan uses against their foes in battle. The true masters of this art command heightened levels of fearful respect from their peers, using their great bubbling vats to create diseases and poxes so contagious and foul that they can devastate entire armies. It is these diabolically talented architects who attend the Foulrain Congregations in battle, working dark blessings upon the Plagueclaw catapult batteries to ensure their absolute lethality.

PLAGUE MONKS

Diseased devotees of the Horned Rat, Plague Monks form the heart of the seething hordes of the Clans Pestilens swarms. Though inherently cowardly like the rest of their race, the Plague Monks' zealotry makes them brave and extremely dangerous in large numbers.

Congregations of Plague Monks spill across the battlefield in a hideous tide. Ragged, robed figures scrabble over and around one another in their eagerness to sink their fangs into flesh. A rank odour heralds this horrific onslaught, while the squeals and gurgled chanting of the Plague Monks presage a hideous death for their foes. Weird religious trappings clang and flap in the winds of battle, scrolls nailed directly into sloughing flesh and unholy icons brandished aloft. As the Plague Monks crash into the enemy lines, their madness only intensifies. Their numbers alone are enough to blunt enemy attacks and overrun defences, while the unnaturally virulent diseases they bring cause enemies to sicken and die in droves.

The weapons these fanatics wield are vectors of plague in their own right. They brandish rusted cleavers and jagged, splintered knives that drip poisonous concoctions, and their fangs and talons are coated with layers of noxious filth. A mere nick or scratch from such a weapon is enough to cause rampant infection to take hold, meaning that those who survive battle with the Clans Pestilens soon shrivel and die if they have suffered even the most superficial of wounds.

Even worse are the arcane weapons of the Bringers-of-the-Word. These spiteful and ambitious beings are the aspirant underlings of the Plague Priests themselves, each attaching himself to the tail of whichever priest he believes can expedite his climb to power. Bringers-of-the-Word further their priestly masters' agendas and are rewarded for their efforts with potent plague scrolls and Books of Woes. When the crabbed and squirming characters of these texts are read aloud they cause the air to curdle, reality to sour and the enemy to rot where they stand.

The battle madness of the Plague Monks not only makes them deadly aggressors, but also lends them a frightening resilience. Beneath their rotting robes and filth-matted pelts, the zealots' hides have been rendered leathery and tough by the cornucopia of diseases they have willingly subjected themselves to. Nerve endings are rotted, or dulled through leprous degeneration. In this way a Plague Monk may easily shrug off even the most agonising pain, at least until they realise the severity of their wounds and their overdeveloped skaven instinct for self-preservation kicks in.

What Plague Monks lack in cunning and guile they more than make up for with blind religious fervour. Compared to most skaven, the warriors of the Clans Pestilens are positively daring. They exhibit a surprising lack of cowardice in the face of battle, danger or sudden loud noises. This is a blessing for all, as when a Plague Monk's glands do let go, their curdled musk of fear has a particularly offensive stench that has been known to make even Rat Ogors baulk. They are still skaven at heart though, and should battle begin to turn against the hordes of the Clans Pestilens, they will cut and run just as quickly as their less feculent kin.

PLAGUE CENSER BEARERS

Plague Censer Bearers are the most deranged and devoted practitioners of their unhinged faith. Wielding fuming flails, these hallucinating lunatics scamper madly into battle and cause untold damage before meeting their end.

The billowing fog that rolls from the censers of the Plague Censer Bearers is inimical to life. Before battle, each large brass censer is carefully filled with noxious concoctions of the Plague Priests' devising. Whether it be pus-soaked incense of pallid rotshade, the disease-bloated hearts of butchered, plague-riddled corpses, thrice-cursed ashes from a victim of a Great Plague or some other fell mixture, the end result is the same. Soaked in warpstone-infused oil and set alight, the contents of the censers belch noxious gases. These blister flesh, corrode metal and cause organs and joints to swell with rancid fluids.

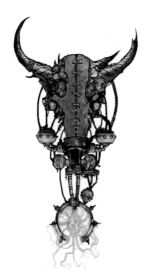

Plague Monks are significantly more resistant to these fumes than other, less corrupt forms of life, but even they will eventually dissolve and die amidst the smog. It is for this reason that only the most

deluded or unfortunate amongst the teeming ranks of the Clans Pestilens find themselves wielding plague censers. Some, those with rotgrubs riddling their brains or frothblight flowing through their arteries, see becoming a Plague Censer Bearer as a true blessing. To such beings, the corrosive vapours emitted by the plague censers only intensify their already feverish hallucinations and strengthen their convictions that the Second Great Withering is underway.

For the majority, though, there is some reticence, at least until the plague fumes cloud their minds and drive them into an insensible killing frenzy. Such wretches are likely to be selected by the Plague Priests from amongst those up-and-coming brethren who might soon become rivals. Set upon by gangs of their peers, these Plague Monks are knocked unconscious, only to wake upon the battlefield with plague censers chained to their handclaws. Others are captives and slaves from different clans, swaddled in filth-caked robes and given the choice between wielding the censer or being used as ingredients for the vile brew inside it.

However they came to be, once the fumes take hold and the battle is at hand, the Plague Censer Bearers become whirling, slavering dervishes. They charge into the enemy lines with no thought for their own safety, ignoring whistling bolts or coruscating blasts of magic as they scurry madly across the battlefield to bludgeon and kill with their horrific weapons.

SEPSKRIK THE FOUL

The Verminlord Corruptor known as Sepskrik the Foul has been responsible for the outbreaks of some of the most horrific plagues in the history of the Mortal Realms. It was he who introduced the Crimsonweal Curse to the fountains of the Glittering City, and who set loose the Grey Shrivelling amid the Everwoods of High Sephardia. Sepskrik is known as the Foul for his pestilent stench and for the living carpet of parasites that seethes over his fur. Yet even though the Verminlord's very presence leaves greasy trails of dark corruption on everything he touches, the daemon is actually a fastidious and obsessive collector of the very finest plague ingredients. Hagwolf teeth must be polished to a fine sheen, rotwater must retain the perfect porridgy consistency, while troggoth warts must be shrivelled to just the right size. The daemon's strange lair is a clinking, creaking repository of alembic jars beyond count, within which float myriad horrors gathered from across the realms, horrors that he has slain entire armies to possess.

PLAGUE FURNACES

The war engines of the Clans Pestilens are more than just weapons; they are the befouled altars at which the Virulent Processions worship, mobile fanes of corruption towards which the Plague Monks direct their devotions. This is most true of the fearsome constructs known as Plague Furnaces.

Plague Furnaces are huge wheeled carriages of rotting wood and rusting metal, heaved into battle by teeming hordes of Plague Monks. Their sheer bulk is deadly in its own right, and many foes are crushed beneath their grinding wheels as the engines are driven forwards. Yet the mass of the Plague Furnace is but the least of the many reasons why the Clans Pestilens' enemies should fear these foul creations.

Each Plague Furnace is ridden to war by a Plague Priest, who uses the furnace as a moving pulpit from which to call down foul curses on the foe and dark blessings upon his allies. Some of the most virulent blights known to the Plague Priests of the Clans Pestilens can only be summoned beneath the pulsating light from a Plague Furnace's runes, and the efficacy of the contagions that the priests unleash is said to be magnified by the Great Corruptor when they are evoked from the platform of such a rolling shrine.

More dangerous still is the great censer at the Plague Furnace's heart. Chunks of raw warpstone are saturated with mixtures of diseased foulness and piled into this massive sphere before being doused with rancid alchemical fluids and set aflame. The resultant toxic smoke billows outwards in waves that drive the devotees of the Clans Pestilens into an ecstatic frenzy even as they cause rapid decomposition and outbreaks of plague amongst the foe.

These enormous censers are swung back and forth by means of chains that are tugged upon by packs of claw-chosen Plague Monks. The monks are lent crazed strength by their zeal, coupled with inhalation of the censer's fumes. Working together, they swing the giant spiked sphere back and forth in an ever more aggressive rhythm until its momentum is unstoppable and every swing emits a low, throaty roar. When the Plague Furnace draws near enough to the foe, the Plague Monks can send the censer rattling forward like a giant wrecking ball to smash down onto a packed regiment, crush a monstrous opponent or shatter fortress gates with a single blow. This motion also sends lethal clouds of plague-smog rolling outwards, engulfing the shell-shocked survivors of the censer's impact in killing vapours. So does the Plague Furnace shatter the heart of enemy battle lines, or bring down the walls of their fastnesses and leave nothing but suppurating corpses in the path of the onrushing skaven hordes.

PLAGUECLAWS

Rotten wood creaks as the throwing arm of the Plagueclaw catapult is cranked slowly back until it strains near to breaking point. Only then are the plagues of the Clans Pestilens loaded into the weapon's claw, the diseases mixed into a rank sludge composed of decaying organic matter and foul effluvia that bubbles and hisses ominously. A single wrench upon a rusted leaver and the vile brew is hurled high into the air before raining down upon the enemy, where it spreads fast-acting and withering contagions to all those it does not immediately dissolve into flesh-slurry.

Rolling at the rear of each pestilent procession, the silhouettes of these rotwood catapults resemble sinister gallows or some species of ghastly stalking insect. They creak forward on mouldering wooden wheels, heaved into position where they can overlook the battlefield like the spectre of death come to rain misery and decay upon the foe.

Plagueclaws are seen by the Clans Pestilens as divine instruments of the Horned Rat's will, the devices by which he bestows pestilence upon the worthy and the unworthy alike. They are potent vectors for plagues so incredibly lethal that they spread like wildfire through armies in the field, fortress garrisons and city populations alike.

The Plague Priests make a great show of calling down the Great Corruptor's blessings upon the cauldrons in which Plagueclaw ammunition is brewed, for to them the act of firing the weapons' payloads into the foe is a ritual of dark baptism that can end battles before they begin and bring sieges to a swift and horrific conclusion. Into the Plagueclaws are ladled the most infectious brews the Plague Priests can conjure and even – on occasions of great moment – precious doses of one or more of the Great Plagues that may be used to infect whole nations from the catalyst of a single battlefield.

Whether lofting their shots high over castle walls or into the midst of a heaving melee, accuracy is of little concern to the Plagueclaw crews. The weapons need only drop their ammunition in the general vicinity of their victims in order to begin an epidemic amongst their ranks. And if a few friendly warriors are caught amidst the splattering salvoes? Well, then those Plague Monks are especially blessed!

It is also seen as a great honour to crew a Plagueclaw, and not only because it allows a skaven to attack his foes from a nice safe remove. Many Plague Monks believe that those who crew these weapons become so saturated with filth that, upon their inevitable and unpleasantly messy deaths from exposure to irresistible plagues, they pass through the veil to become one with the Great Corruptor.

THE FERVID FANG

The Plague Monks of the Fervid Fang fought in many great battles during the War of Life. They surged against the walls of the greenhold of Yillith and hacked their way through the bladebowers to devour the Sylvaneth soulpods beyond. They fought alongside, and then – once their duplicitous trap was sprung – against the Rotbringer Cysts of Lord Gortulpus the Thrice-spattered. They even followed the cloven hoof-tread of the Verminlord Corruptor Threxiphane the Malignificant, all the way up the Vinecoil and through the spore-storms to tear the beating heart from the Jade Kingdom of Eyshir. Normally, such a history of endless slaughter would have seen a clawpack of Plague Monks annihilated, yet the Fervid Fang are infected with a rare strain of groansplice pox – no matter what violence is done to them, so long as their festering hearts are not destroyed these Plague Monks will slowly – and revoltingly – regrow and regenerate their ravaged flesh. This process of foul rebirth has left the Fervid Fang raving mad, for it is agonising and hideous, yet still they fight on.

WARRIORS OF VERMINUS

Where other Great Clans base their power upon twisted ingenuity or strange arts of war, the Clans Verminus rely upon sheer numbers. It is a strategy that has served them well, as attested by their warriors' presence in the vast majority of skaven swarms, and the trail of enemies they have left as nothing more than gnawed bones.

CLAWLORDS

In battle, Clawlords fight with the same merciless and underhanded savagery with which they have climbed the rungs of skaven society, seizing upon the slightest advantage that may offer victory. Though swaggering and toweringly arrogant, Verminus Clawlords share – perhaps even epitomise – their race's instinct for self-preservation; they will not think twice about stooping to any depths in order to murder their foes while remaining alive themselves. Whether it be blowing warpstone dust into an enemy's eyes to blind them, hurling a hapless lackey into their foe's path, dropping a massive stalactite on their opponent or any number of other devious tactics; if it wins the fight, a Clawlord will try it in a heartbeat.

The status of Clawlord is not something that a skaven works towards and earns, but rather something that is seized in a bloody instant. Rivals must be butchered without mercy. Some would-be Clawlords arrange unfortunate accidents for their opponents; whether they are crushed by a collapsing tunnel, carelessly impale themselves upon a clawful of throwing daggers, succumb to mysteriously poisoned meat, find themselves on the wrong end of a misfiring warpfire thrower or whatever else, death can come suddenly and with a remarkable sense of timing.

Other aspirants are less subtle, calling out their rivals amidst much snarling and baring of chisel-like incisors, overcoming them in bloody one-on-one combat and then devouring their corpses in front of their horrified underlings. However they come to power, the real battle for a Clawlord is holding onto it. Manipulation, the ability to set rivals against one another and retaining the loyalty of those who would murder him in a heartbeat are all skills a Clawlord must possess if

he wishes to survive. Any threats to a leader's position must be ruthlessly countered, and no effort is spared in eliminating potential usurpers. Meanwhile, conquests and victories must be constantly accrued if a Clawlord wishes to minimise the muttering of detractors. Many in skavendom believe this is one of the main reasons the Clans Verminus are so perpetually aggressive – the Clawlords always need new trophies, and will spend as many of their fellows' lives as they must to acquire them.

CLANRATS

The main body of many skaven swarms is formed of Clanrats – the vast and flea-bitten hordes of ratmen that make up the bulk of the Clans Verminus. In all the underground burrows, strongholds and teeming cavern-cities that constitute the Under-Empire, only the worker dregs and slaves are more numerous.

Individually, Clanrats are not natural warriors. Their weapons and armour are typically rusty and poorly maintained, often scavenged from fallen or murdered comrades. They are ill-disciplined, cowardly and prone to infighting. However, Clanrats are fast and vicious, and when they gather in large numbers they become exponentially more dangerous.

Sweeping forward in seething hordes, the Clanrats overwhelm their enemies, biting, stabbing, screeching, squirting the musk of fear and trampling their own fallen beneath their bloody claws. Hundreds of Clanrats inevitably fall in any determined assault, but this just means more rivals slain and better scavenging rights for the survivors. It also ensures a ready source of food – so hyperactive are the metabolisms of skaven that, after sufficiently frantic exertion, they succumb to a ravenous mania known as the black hunger. Once pushed to

this near-mindless state, they must either consume sufficient flesh to sate themselves, or else perish as they are gnawed away from within. Thus the fallen of both sides soon become naught but meat for the surviving Clanrats come battle's end.

STORMVERMIN

The Stormvermin are the fighting elite of the Clans Verminus. They are distinguishable from their scrawnier litter-mates, often standing a full head taller, with thick, muscular necks and a powerful build. They are marked from birth by their stature, their dark-hued fur and their willingness to savagely dominate the lesser skaven around them.

Stormvermin clawpacks are outfitted with the best gear of war in their clan's armoury. Their duties may include forming a retinue or bodyguard for Clawlords, standing sentry over crucial clan assets – armouries, food stores, breeder pens and the like – or being deployed as vanguard line-breakers, enforcers and shock troops.

In return, Stormvermin revel in their favoured status, reserving the right to feed first upon the fallen from battle – or any insolent enough to attempt to do so before them – and being assigned their own slaves and warrens to lord over.

The services of Stormvermin are often bought by other clans who value their muscle and sheer savagery. They are especially popular as bodyguards, with every ratman of rank, from Grey Seers to Master Moulders to Arch-Warlocks, hiring their own pack of arrogant, bullying Stormvermin to show off their might and importance. Of course, such Stormvermin may well remain loyal to the Verminus clan of their birth, and more than one preening skaven dignitary has met their end skewered upon or hacked to pieces by the blades of their bodyguards' halberds.

HAKKRIT'S FORGEFANGS

Though they have war-warrens dotted throughout skavendom – not least amidst the endless sprawl of Blight City itself – the ultimate stronghold of the mighty Verminus Clan Fang can be found in Chamon. Above the Quenched Lands in Odrenn rises a mountain known as Gildpeak, and there, amidst the ruins of Karak-a-Zaruk, the burrows of Clan Fang proliferate. With hired help from the Clans Skryre, Lord Hakkrit has been able to breathe a corrupted form of life into the ancient duardin forges of that once-noble stronghold, and it is with the aid of tainted rune-magics that he has created his Forgefangs. This band of elite Stormvermin wear heavy armour engraved with jagged skaven runes of spite, and their blades glow with ensorcelled power. Green sparks fly as the Forgefangs duel with their enemies, each strike and counter-strike loosing arcs of warp lightning that blast the enemy to cinders. Strutting at the head of this scorched and arrogant bodyguard, Clawlord Hakkrit carves down all who dare to stand in his magnificent path.

MONSTERS OF MOULDER

Flesh-twisters and monster-makers beyond compare, the Clans Moulder are ghoulish beastmasters whose power stems from the grotesque living weapons that crawl from their spawning pits. With lash and goad do their Packmasters drive their verminous monsters into battle, then delight in watching them tear the enemy to shreds.

MASTER MOULDERS
Deranged experts in beast breeding and warpstone-triggered mutation, the Master Moulders hold absolute power over their clans. Brutish, conniving and vicious, they have come to resemble the very monsters they create. Many have been mutated by constant exposure to warpstone, or in some cases even self-experimentation. They boast bulked-up musculatures, additional limbs, monstrous visages and ferocious metabolisms that require them to constantly devour living flesh. Master Moulders wield whistling lashes and huge, spring-loaded pole arms known as things-catchers in battle, but their real weapons are the monstrous creatures that they raise and unleash upon the foe.

PACKMASTERS
The mutated fighting beasts made by the Clans Moulder are driven into battle by Packmasters. These cruel skaven are experts at goading their ferocious charges into battle, ensuring that the beasts are sufficiently riled when they reach the foe's lines. Packmasters ply their whips and things-catchers with savage skill, for any who fail to do so are soon devoured by the beasts they seek to master.

The notorious Fiendmongers of Clan Snirk are a band of Packmasters who well understand the value of psychological warfare. The beasts they breed are amongst the ghastliest of all Moulder's creations.

WAR RATS
Rats of every size are unleashed by the Clans Moulder. The smallest flow across the battlefield in huge and voracious swarms. The larger beasts, some reaching the size of hunting hounds, launch themselves at the enemy in waves and can drag down even the most accomplished warriors through sheer weight of numbers.

RAT OGORS
These hulking monsters are arguably the Clans Moulder's most successful breed of war beast. Horrific fusions of skaven and ogor, they are stitched, melded and – in some cases – vat grown through a mixture of cryptosurgery and sorcery. Warpstone balms make obscene fusions of normally incompatible anatomies possible, and forge hugely muscled, rabidly ferocious and extremely stupid monsters. Driven into battle at the head of Moulder swarms or sold off to other clans for obscene prices, these berserk monstrosities rip through the enemy ranks in sprays of blood and viscera, and can break entire enemy armies with their fury.

HELL PIT ABOMINATIONS
The Hell Pit Abomination is a living mountain of misshapen flesh, the product of warpstone-fuelled grafting of many monstrous beasts into a single unholy whole. The creature moves in a revolting, undulating motion, its myriad limbs clawing and dragging, its wheeled carriage groaning under the strain of its bloated, stinking flesh. It hunts by scent, sound and vibration, slither-shambling as quickly as it can towards its prey. Those who do not flee in terror find themselves facing a looming mass of scabrous muscle and blubber that rears high before slamming down to crush them flat. Maws snap, talons lash, bludgeons pulverise, and another mound of mangled corpses is left in the Abomination's wake.

AGENTS OF ESHIN

Stealth, misdirection and a sudden, agonising death – these are the hallmarks of Eshin. Their clans lurk in the shadows and hire themselves out as spies and assassins. Yet they have their own warriors, their own weapons and ways of war, and their numbers are far greater than even their most paranoid rivals might dread.

DEATHMASTERS

Though the true masters of the Clans Eshin rarely emerge from the Realm of Shadow, all of skavendom know to fear their strong left claws, the Deathmasters. Little is known about these elite agents beyond rumour and fear. It is said that they can slither through cracks no wider than a hair, that their very shadows are poisonous, and that they can communicate silently with one another within their minds. Certainly, their mastery of the arts of swift and stealthy murder are remarkable. Deathmasters can leap many times their own height, can run along vertical surfaces, and duck and weave so fast that even the most skilled warriors find it impossible to land a telling blow on them. They can detect and identify venoms by smell alone, catch hurtling projectiles out of thin air, and are as deadly with their bare claws as most veteran killers are with their favourite weapon.

Of course, Deathmasters do not practise unarmed combat exclusively. A bewildering array of blades, throwing weapons, poisons, explosives and more esoteric tools are theirs to wield as they see fit. Arson, sabotage, assassination and misdirection – all lie within their remit. The Clans Eshin entrust their Deathmasters with almost complete autonomy when it comes to the manner in which they complete their secretive missions, and these clandestine skaven are all the more effective for it.

GUTTER RUNNERS

The Gutter Runners form the black-clad death squads of the Clans Eshin. Having proven themselves amongst the ranks of the Night Runners, they are claw-picked by their masters to be initiated into the deeper mysteries of Eshin. Alone amongst the Great Clans, a skaven must earn the right to progress through the Eshin ranks. This does not stop countless aspirants from trying to trick or murder their way to the top, of course, but such fools are rarely heard from again.

Gutter Runners are adept at both armed and unarmed combat. They serve as scouts and saboteurs, often softening up the enemy before battle begins by spiking guns, murdering key personnel, stealing plans, poisoning rations and otherwise causing mayhem. Once the real fight begins, they slip through the carnage like half-seen ghosts, striking wherever the foe is weakest before fading away to attack again elsewhere.

NIGHT RUNNERS

Night Runners make up the bulk of the Clans Eshin. They slink furtively around their enemies' flanks and encircle their rear before striking with vicious aggression. Night Runners hurl volleys of throwing stars and sling-stones to panic and weaken the foe, then fall upon them with fangs and flashing blades. Wherever possible, they aim for their targets' vulnerable spots, seeking to do as much damage as they can as quickly as they can. If they do not swiftly overrun their enemies the Night Runners will scurry away, ready to strike again from another angle.

The Thirteenth Blade is a Slinktalon belonging to Eshin Clan Stryk. Each skaven must brew and then prove the lethality of a unique poison for his blades in order to earn a place in their ranks.

Delving for secrets of the past, the Kharadron Overlords break open an ancient karak. Instead of riches, they are confronted by a seething tide of murderous skaven boiling up from the depths.

COLOURS OF RUIN

From crackling warp lightning and gleaming fangs, to the sheer number of verminous foot soldiers flooding the battlefield, skaven swarms are as impressive as they are fearsome. Here we present a showcase of skaven Citadel Miniatures expertly painted by Games Workshop's very own 'Eavy Metal Team and Design Studio army painters.

Taking up a commanding position at the heart of his swarm, a Clawlord shrieks orders at his teeming underlings. In the shadows around him, the agents of the Masterclan watch with glee as their twisted agendas are fulfilled.

Grey Seer

Clawlord

Warlock Bombardier

Grey Seer Thanquol on Boneripper

A Grey Seer summons the Bell of Doom to spread terror through the Beastclaw Raiders' lines.

Plague Censer Bearer

Plague Priest

Plague Monk

Bringer-of-the-Word

Contagion Banner Bearer

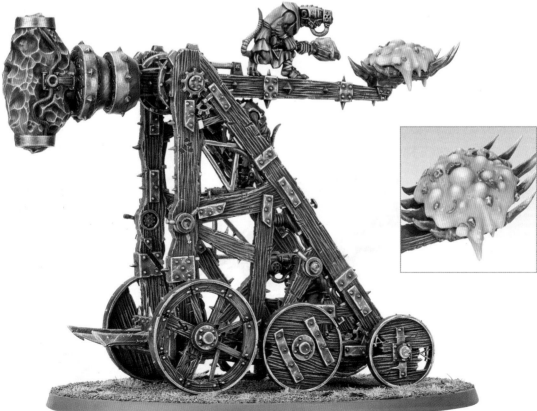

Plagueclaw

Plague Priest on Plague Furnace

A Verminlord Corruptor leads the Clans Pestilens in a frenzied charge against the Fyreslayers.

A Warlock Bombardier watches from a lofty perch as his swarm scurries out to war.

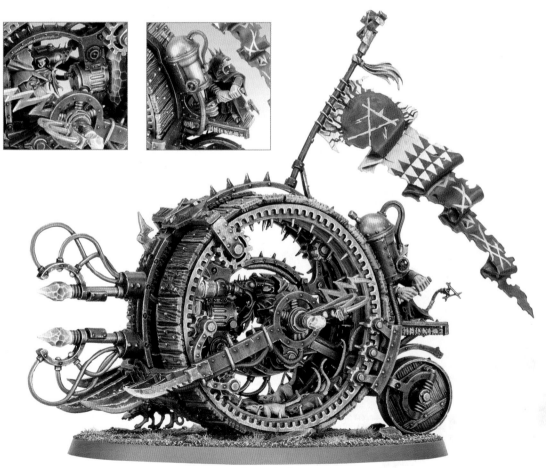

Doomwheel

Skryre Acolyte *Arch-Warlock* *Warp-Grinder*

The Clans Skryre battle the Kharadron Overlords in the fume-filled depths.

Warp Lightning Cannon

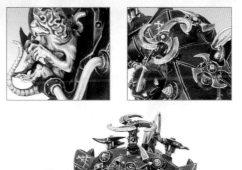

Stormfiend with Grinderfists

Stormfiend with Doomflayer Gauntlets and Warpstone-laced Armour

An Eshin Deathmaster lurks upon a high platform, poised to eliminate the luckless foes passing below.

A Verminlord Deceiver bursts from the shadows to strike down a Lord-Arcanum.

Clanrat of Verminus
Clan Fang

Clanrat hired by Eshin
Clan Stryk

Clanrat hired by
Moulder Clan Dregg

Clanrat hired by
Pestilens Clan Vomikrit

Clanrat of Verminus
Clan Stabbik

Stormvermin of Verminus
Clan Skarrik

Stormvermin hired by
Moulder Clan Threbb

Stormvermin hired by Eshin
Clan Nichtus

Stormvermin hired by
Moulder Clan Ghrubbitus

A Clawlord of Clan Morskrit exhorts his warriors into battle from a vantage point well out of harm's way.

A Master Moulder of Clan Dregg drives his Rat Ogors towards the enemy.

THE FELLTALON SWARM

Whether they be anarchic assemblages of war engines and horrific monsters, or vast hordes consisting of clawpack after clawpack of infantry, skaven armies are always fearsome and impressive. There are many ways to collect a swarm; this spread offers just one example of how to muster the Children of the Horned Rat for war.

This imposing skaven swarm represents an army of the Clans Verminus, supported by copious hireling assets from the Clans Moulder and Skryre, all manipulated and driven on by the devious agents of the Masterclan. At its head stalks the terrifying form of the Verminlord Warpseer Skrivezzyk, of whom all other skaven in the army live in fear. The swarm's general and Verminus warleader is Clawlord Skrakh, who is advised – usually against his will – by the devious Grey Seer Hyskrik, who rides to war atop his Screaming Bell.

A conclave of Skryre warlocks leads their own portion of the force into battle, with Arch-Warlock Sparkgnaw lording it over Warlock Engineer Thryk and Warlock Bombardier Thraskus. The beast packs of Moulder, meanwhile, are driven into battle by the lash of Master Moulder Stitchgut.

Though they spend much of their time back-stabbing, baiting and politicking against one another, these vicious and ambitious leaders hold the swarm together and direct it with lethal effect against the foe.

The core of Skrakh's swarm comprises three clawpacks of Clanrats – the Fang-gougers, the Masterful Things-Slayers and Retchfang's Conquerors – and two sizeable clawpacks of Stormvermin: Bladeclaw's Much-Fearsome Warbringers and Skartail's Kill-Kill Verminguard. The sheer massed numbers of these infantry units are enough to overrun the enemy's battle line, or at the least pin the foe in place while the army's more powerful elements manoeuvre into position. After all, every one of these skaven warriors is expendable…

Serving to keep their bestial creations in line, a small group of Packmasters goads vicious Giant Rats into battle on the army's flank. Skryre Acolytes scurry around the other, the self-titled Gas-choke Lungflayers hurling their poisoned wind globes at targets of opportunity. Meanwhile, a great menagerie of twisted Moulder beasts ploughs directly into the foe; Rat Swarms scrabble up legs and sink chisel fangs into exposed flesh, right before bellowing Rat Ogors smash a bloody path through the enemy's ranks. Worse follows, the ground shuddering as the vast form of the Hell Pit Abomination known simply as the Maw-Terror squirms and rends its way through the shell-shocked survivors, leaving nothing but the gory ruin of its crushed victims in its wake.

Not to be outdone, the Skryre Jezzail teams of the Long-Far Kill-Slayers unleash volley after volley of warpstone shot. Panic spreads as ever more warriors are cut down, and then the Stormfiends hit home; two lumbering clawpacks, the Rattle-Rip Beasts and Thryk's Verminous Onslaught, blast and smash everything before them, laying waste to massed enemy regiments and monstrous opponents with equal ease.

One more, mighty figure looms at the heart of this swarm. Did Grey Seer Thanquol muster this force? Is he, in fact, its true master? Or is he simply capitalising upon its presence to further his own deranged agendas before leaving it to be annihilated in his wake? Only the Horned Rat knows for sure…

1. Verminlord Warpseer
2. Clawlord
3. Grey Seer on Screaming Bell
4. Arch-Warlock
5. Warlock Engineer
6. Warlock Bombardier
7. Master Moulder
8. Clanrats
9. Clanrats
10. Clanrats
11. Stormvermin
12. Stormvermin
13. Packmasters
14. Giant Rats
15. Skryre Acolytes
16. Rat Swarms
17. Rat Ogors
18. Hell Pit Abomination
19. Jezzails
20. Stormfiends
21. Stormfiends
22. Doom-Flayer
23. Thanquol on Boneripper

61

PAINTING YOUR SKAVEN CLANS

A skaven army is an exciting painting challenge no matter whether you are a veteran hobbyist or you have never picked up a paintbrush in your life. On the following pages you will find stage-by-stage guides to help you get the most of your skaven Citadel Miniatures, with tips and examples from the experts.

The skaven are one of the largest and most varied miniatures ranges produced by Games Workshop. From fleshy monsters with vicious fangs and scabrous fur, to clanking mechanical war engines, diseased Plague Monks in rotting robes and serried ranks of armoured Stormvermin, there is an enormous amount of personal choice in what sorts of aesthetics, textures and details your collection will feature. This, coupled with the sheer number of skaven that makes up a swarm, may seem a little daunting at first. However, with the help of the tips and tricks on the following pages you will soon find yourself building up a skaventide worthy of the Horned Rat himself!

Painting your Citadel Miniatures is an enjoyable part of the Games Workshop hobby, and a way to truly personalise your collection. Whether you choose to copy the colour schemes shown in this battletome or to invent your own, wholly unique clan colour scheme, when you put a fully painted army on the tabletop the effect is always spectacular. Some painters enjoy lavishing hours of time and attention on each model, teasing out every last detail to the highest possible standard. Others prefer powering through batches of miniatures, getting them painted to a neat and basic standard, the better to quickly finish their army and start rolling dice. As with all aspects of this hobby, there's really no right or wrong way to do things as long as you're happy with the end result. So whether you're looking to paint up a claw-picked selection of your favourite skaven miniatures

or gather a much-mighty swarm and overrun the Mortal Realms, these pages contain invaluable information on how to go about painting everything from skaven skin and fur to glowing warpstone, dripping poison and diseased slime!

WARHAMMER TV

Warhammer TV's painting tutorials have insights for everyone, as they show you how to paint Citadel Miniatures from start to finish. The guides are available for free on games-workshop.com, and can also be watched via the Warhammer TV YouTube channel. Why not take a moment to check them out?

SKIN

  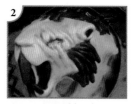 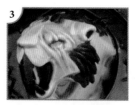

1 Start by applying a basecoat consisting of two thin coats of Cadian Fleshtone.

2 Next, mix Reikland Fleshshade with Lahmian Medium and apply it all over the skin areas.

3 Paint the raised areas of the skin with Kislev Flesh, being careful to avoid the shading in the recesses.

4 On larger models, define the edges and extremities with highlights of Flayed One Flesh.

CLOTH

Basecoat Mephiston Red, shade Nuln Oil, layer Evil Sunz Scarlet, highlight Fire Dragon Bright.

Basecoat Straken Green, shade Biel-Tan Green, layer Nurgling Green, highlight Screaming Skull.

Rakarth Flesh, Seraphim Sepia, Pallid Wych Flesh, Steel Legion Drab drybrush.

Basecoat Incubi Darkness, shade Nuln Oil, layer Sybarite Green, highlight Dawnstone.

FUR

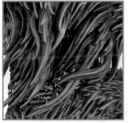   

Basecoat Mournfang Brown, shade Agrax Earthshade, layer Skrag Brown, highlight Tau Light Ochre.

Basecoat Abaddon Black, then apply increasingly fine highlights of Eshin Grey, Dawnstone, then Administratum Grey.

Basecoat Pallid Wych Flesh, shade Casandora Yellow, highlight with Pallid Wych Flesh, then apply a fine highlight of White Scar.

Basecoat Rhinox Hide, shade Nuln Oil, drybrush with Mournfang Brown, then apply a light drybrush of XV88.

BLUE ARMOUR

1 Start by applying a basecoat of Stegadon Scale Green to the armoured areas of the model.

2 Next, paint Agrax Earthshade into the recesses of the armour and between the plates.

3 Once the shade has dried fully, apply thick edge highlights of Thunderhawk Blue.

4 Finally, apply fine highlights of Fenrisian Grey to the edges of the armour plates.

BANNERS

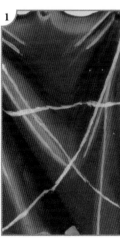   

1 In order to paint the Clan Fang rune onto your banners, begin by painting three 'guide lines' in the desired colour. You will use these as a frame around which to paint the rune itself.

2 Once your guide lines are dry, carefully develop each one into a full shape using the same colour. Be careful to keep your brushwork neat and the course of the shapes consistent over the ripples on the banner.

3 Now, repeat the first two steps with the smaller intersecting lines on the top right-hand part of the Clan Fang rune.

4 To apply scratches to the design, simply stipple or dab small dots of the banner's basecoat colour onto the rune. You can also use this stage to tidy up any mistakes along the edges of your rune with the banner's base colour as required.

SKAVEN BLADES

For a warpstone blade, start by basecoating the blade with Caliban Green. Next, pick out the hard edges of the blade with Warpstone Green. To finish, apply a finer edge highlight of Moot Green, then an even finer edge highlight of Yriel Yellow.

To paint rusted blades, begin with a basecoat of Leadbelcher. Apply a shade of Agrax Earthshade then, when this is dry, an edge highlight of Stormhost Silver to the edges. Finally, stipple some Ryza Rust onto the blade in patches.

Start with a Leadbelcher basecoat. Next, mix Mournfang Brown and Sotek Green, water it down, and apply it as a thin glaze. Shade the blade with Agrax Earthshade, then edge highlight with Stormhost Silver.

This blade was basecoated with Ironbreaker, shaded with Agrax Earthshade and edge highlighted with Stormhost Silver. The poison was basecoated using Caliban Green, then highlighted with Warpstone Glow, Moot Green and Yriel Yellow.

SKAVEN DETAILS

For fangs and talons, basecoat XV88, layer Balor Brown, then highlight Screaming Skull.

When painting tails, darken them by applying several thin glazes of Screamer Pink.

Basecoat Celestra Grey, glaze Waywatcher Green, shade Biel-Tan Green toward the source of the smoke, then highlight with Ulthuan Grey then White Scar.

Basecoat Hashut Copper, shade Reikland Fleshshade, layer Sycorax Bronze, highlight Stormhost Silver, then apply Nihilak Oxide for verdigris.

To paint the vile plague-slop loaded into the Plagueclaw, start with an Ushabti Bone basecoat. Apply a thin glaze of Lamenters Yellow, then a thinned wash of Athonian Camoshade. Water down and re-apply thinned Ushabti Bone, then highlight with Pallid Wych Flesh.

For horns, basecoat with Baneblade Brown. Next, water down Daemonette Hide and apply as a thin glaze, then do the same with Abaddon Black, especially towards the horns' tips. Finish by applying highlights of Rakarth Flesh, then Pallid Wych Flesh.

For skaven wood, basecoat with Rhinox Hide then apply a shade of Nuln Oil. Once this has dried, apply a drybrush of Gorthor Brown, then a lighter drybrush of Karak Stone. To make it look as though mould is growing in the cracks, apply patches of Biel-Tan Green.

BANNERS AND DESIGNS

Basecoat Mephiston Red. Use Nuln Oil to shade the folds and holes, and to paint dirty patches. Layer with Evil Sunz Scarlet, then highlight with Fire Dragon Bright.

First, paint the banner Caliban Green. Build up the vivid design with Warpstone Glow, then outline it with Moot Green. Use White Scar for the rune.

Skaven use jagged runes that often resemble claw-marks, gouged wounds and the like. These have been painted on free-hand using Rakarth Flesh.

Start with a basecoat of Kantor Blue, then apply a layer of Caledor Blue. Paint the triangles using Fenrisian Grey, then highlight the edges with Ulthuan Grey.

WARPSTONE

1

To paint warpstone, start by applying a Caliban Green basecoat.

2

Once the basecoat is dry, apply thick, chunky highlights of Warpstone Glow as shown.

3

Now, pick out the raised areas with a much finer highlight of Moot Green to make the edges appear to glow.

4

Lastly, apply gentle accents of Yriel Yellow to the sharp points and selected raised edges.

ARMOUR VARIANTS

To paint red armour plates, start with a basecoat of Mephiston Red. Shade the recesses with Nuln Oil, then highlight the edges with Evil Sunz Scarlet. Finish with a fine edge highlight of Fire Dragon Bright.

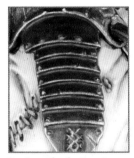

Begin with a basecoat of Warplock Bronze. Drybrush with Runelord Brass, then highlight the edges of the plates with Ironbreaker. Lastly, use Nihilakh Oxide in the recesses to give a verdigris look.

For black armour, start with an Abaddon Black basecoat. Apply chunky highlights of Eshin Grey, followed by progressively finer highlights of Dawnstone then Administratum Grey.

For this green armour, start with a basecoat of Waaagh! Flesh, then shade with Nuln Oil. Apply a chunky highlight of Loren Forest, then pick out the edges of the plates with an Elysian Green fine highlight.

THE SKAVENTIDE

This battletome contains all of the rules you need to field your skaven miniatures on the battlefields of the Mortal Realms, from a host of exciting allegiance abilities to a range of warscrolls and warscroll battalions. The rules are split into the following sections.

ALLEGIANCE ABILITIES

This section describes the allegiance abilities available to a Skaventide army. The rules for how to use the following allegiance abilities can be found in the core rules.

BATTLE TRAITS

Abilities available to every unit in a Skaventide army (pg 67-68).

COMMAND TRAITS

Abilities available to the general of a Skaventide army if it is a **Hero** (pg 69).

ARTEFACTS OF POWER

Artefacts available to **Heroes** in a Skaventide army (pg 72-77).

SPELL LORES

Spells available to **Wizards** in a Skaventide army (pg 78-79).

GNAWHOLES

Here you will find the rules and scenery warscroll for the Gnawhole terrain feature (pg 80-81).

BATTLEPLANS

This section includes new narrative battleplans that can be played with a Skaventide army (pg 82-85).

PATH TO GLORY

This section contains rules for using your skaven collection in Path to Glory campaigns (pg 86-90).

WARSCROLLS

This section includes all of the warscrolls you will need to play games of Warhammer Age of Sigmar with your skaven miniatures.

There are three types of warscroll included in this section:

WARSCROLL BATTALIONS

These are formations made up of several Skaventide units that combine their strengths to gain powerful new abilities (pg 92-98).

WARSCROLLS

A warscroll for each unit is included here. The rules for using a Skaventide unit, along with its characteristics and abilities, are detailed on its warscroll (pg 99-124).

ENDLESS SPELL WARSCROLLS

There are three endless spell warscrolls that detail the rules for unique and powerful spells that can be summoned by Skaventide **Wizards** (pg 125-126). The rules for playing games with endless spells can be found in the *Warhammer Age of Sigmar Core Book*, and in *Warhammer Age of Sigmar: Malign Sorcery*.

PITCHED BATTLE PROFILES

This section contains Pitched Battle profiles for the units, warscroll battalions and endless spells in this book (pg 127-128).

ALLIES

This section has a list of the allies a Skaventide army can include (pg 128).

ALLEGIANCE ABILITIES
BATTLE TRAITS

TEACHINGS OF THE HORNED RAT

LEAD FROM THE BACK

In skaven society, the rear of a formation is a position of honour and leadership. Not least, this is so that skaven rulers can use their underlings as a living shield.

The Look Out, Sir! rule applies to an attack made with a melee weapon as well as an attack made with a missile weapon if the target of the attack is a **Skaventide Hero** that is not a **Monster**.

SCURRY AWAY

To the skaven, prudent cowardice is a virtue, and their leaders do not think twice about scurrying off when the going gets too dangerous.

In the combat phase, when you pick a friendly **Skaventide Hero** to fight with, you can say it is going to scurry away instead of making a pile-in move and then attacking. If you do so, that **Hero** must make a normal move, and must retreat.

OVERWHELMING MASS

Facing the onslaught of massed skaven clawpacks is akin to being buried alive by an avalanche of furry flesh, stabbing blades and gnashing chisel fangs.

Add 1 to hit rolls for attacks made with melee weapons by **Skaventide** units while they have 20 or more models. In addition, add 1 to wound rolls for attacks made with melee weapons by **Skaventide** units while they have 30 or more models.

STRENGTH IN NUMBERS

Skaven are not brave by nature, but do take courage from being in large packs.

When a **Skaventide** unit takes a battleshock test, add 2 to its Bravery characteristic instead of 1 for every 10 models in the unit.

WAYS OF THE GREAT CLANS

MASTERCLAN – SKILLED MANIPULATORS

Even amongst a race as devious and self-serving as the skaven, there are those with minds so cunning and labyrinthine that they are able to manipulate the rest into doing their bidding.

Each time a friendly **Masterclan** model uses a command ability, roll a dice. On a 5+ you receive 1 extra command point.

MOULDER – PRIZED CREATIONS

Master Moulders constantly strive to improve their breeding stock with ever more powerful mutations and modifications, and their most successful creations are highly prized.

At the start of the first battle round, before determining which player has the first turn, you can pick 1 friendly **Clans Moulder Fighting Beast** model for each **Master Moulder** in your army. The same **Fighting Beast** cannot be picked more than once to benefit from this ability. Add D3 to the Wounds characteristic of each of those models (roll separately for each). In addition, you can re-roll hit rolls of 1 for attacks made with melee weapons by those models.

ESHIN – MASTERS OF MURDER

The elite agents of the Clans Eshin are credited with all manner of terrifying supernatural abilities in the field of assassination. Once they have chosen their prey, their victims stand little chance of escape…

If your army includes any **Clans Eshin Heroes**, at the start of the first battle round, before determining which player has the first turn, you can pick 1 enemy **Hero** for each **Clans Eshin Hero** in your army. You can re-roll wound rolls for attacks made by friendly **Clans Eshin** units that target those enemy **Heroes** in that battle.

VERMINUS – MIGHTY WARLORDS

A Clawlord must seize control by ruthless force, proving themselves to be both an apex fighter and a devious adversary who their rivals would do well to fear.

When you pick command traits, you can pick 1 command trait for up to 6 friendly **Clawlords**, in addition to 1 command trait for your general if your general is not a **Clawlord**. You must pick a different command trait for each **Clawlord** that has a command trait, and no model can have more than 1 command trait. You can use the command trait for that **Clawlord** even though they are not your general.

SKRYE – WARPSTONE SPARKS

Warpstone sparks are small canisters of caged warp lightning that can be slotted into the strange inventions carried by the warlocks of the Clans Skryre. They are used to catalyse the flow of magic and improve the potency of skaven weapons, their energies crackling through wires and conduits to supercharge spells and wreathe blades in coruscating green force. The use of warpstone sparks is dangerous, for explosive malfunctions are always a risk, but the quick road to power is an irresistible lure for any skaven.

If your army includes any **Clans Skryre Heroes**, at the start of the battle, before either army is set up, you can roll a D3 and add 3 to the roll. The result is the number of warpstone sparks that you can use during the battle. You cannot use more than 1 warpstone spark in the same phase.

Each warpstone spark can be used once per battle to carry out 1 of the following warpstone spark abilities:

- In the hero phase, pick 1 friendly **Clans Skryre Wizard**. You can re-roll casting, dispelling and unbinding rolls for that **Wizard** until the end of that phase. At the end of that phase, roll a dice. On a 1, that **Wizard** suffers D3 mortal wounds.

- In your shooting phase, pick 1 friendly **Clans Skryre Hero**. Then pick up to 3 different friendly **Clans Skryre** units that are wholly within 13" of that **Hero**. You can add 1 to the Damage characteristic of missile weapons used by those units until the end of that phase. At the end of that phase, roll a dice. On a 1, that **Hero** suffers D3 mortal wounds.

- In the combat phase, pick 1 friendly **Clans Skryre Hero**. You can re-roll hit rolls for that **Hero** until the end of that phase. At the end of that phase, roll a dice. On a 1, that **Hero** suffers D3 mortal wounds.

PESTILENS – ECHOES OF THE GREAT PLAGUES

Sometimes, the raving prayers of Pestilens priests cause one of the legendary Great Plagues to temporarily manifest upon the battlefield.

If the unmodified prayer roll for a prayer chanted by a friendly **Clans Pestilens Priest** is 6, you can pick 1 of the following Great Plagues to manifest (in addition to the effect of the prayer). Each Great Plague can only manifest once per battle, and no more than one Great Plague can manifest in the same turn.

Bubonic Blightplague: If this Great Plague manifests, pick the nearest enemy unit within 13" of the **Priest** chanting the prayer. That unit is infected with the Bubonic Blightplague. If several enemy units are equally close, you can pick which is infected. The infected unit suffers D6 mortal wounds. If the infected unit is destroyed by these mortal wounds, you can pick another enemy unit within 6" of the last model to be slain from the infected unit. The new unit is infected and suffers D3 mortal wounds. If the second unit is also destroyed, then another enemy unit within 6" of the last model to be slain suffers D3 mortal wounds, and so on until a unit is not destroyed by the disease or there are no other enemy units within 6" when a unit is destroyed.

Crimsonweal Curse: If this Great Plague manifests, pick the nearest enemy unit within 13" of the **Priest** chanting the prayer. That unit is infected with the Crimsonweal Curse. If several enemy units are equally close, you can pick which is infected. The infected unit suffers 1 mortal wound. In addition, at the start of each of your hero phases, the infected unit, and each enemy unit within 1" of the infected unit, suffers 1 mortal wound.

Redmaw Plague: If this Great Plague manifests, pick the nearest enemy **Hero** within 13" of the **Priest** chanting the prayer. That **Hero** is infected with the Redmaw Plague. If several enemy **Heroes** are equally close, you can pick which is infected. If a **Hero** infected with the Redmaw Plague is within 3" of any other models from its own army at the start of any combat phase, and is not within 3" of any models from your army, then you can treat that **Hero** as a friendly model until the end of that combat phase.

The Neverplague: If this Great Plague manifests, you can re-roll prayer rolls for friendly **Clans Pestilens Priests** for the rest of the battle.

Undulant Scourge: If this Great Plague manifests, pick the nearest enemy unit within 13" of the **Priest** chanting the prayer, and roll 1 dice for each model in that unit. If several enemy units are equally close, you can pick which of those units to roll dice for. For each 5+ that unit suffers 1 mortal wound.

COMMAND TRAITS

CUNNING MACHINATIONS
MASTERCLAN HERO only.

D6 Command Trait

1 Malevolent: *Spite and hatred drive this warlord to ever greater heights of violence.*

You can re-roll wound rolls of 1 for attacks made with melee weapons by this general.

2 Verminous Valour: *This vicious rat inspires his followers to commit terrible acts of self-sacrifice.*

Before you allocate a wound or mortal wound to this general, you can roll a dice. Subtract 1 from the roll if this general is a **MONSTER** or **WAR MACHINE**. On a 4+, instead of allocating the wound or mortal wound to this general, you can allocate it to a friendly **SKAVENTIDE** unit within 3" of this general.

3 Savage Overlord: *This warlord punishes his minions' transgressions with savage brutality.*

Add 1 to the Bravery characteristic of friendly **SKAVENTIDE** units while they are wholly within 18" of this general.

4 Supreme Manipulator: *Few amongst even the Masterclan rival this general's ability to exploit his minions.*

You can re-roll the dice that determines if you receive 1 extra command point when you use the Skilled Manipulators battle trait after this general uses a command ability.

5 Master of Magic: *This general is a superlative practitioner of the spellcaster's art.*

Once per hero phase, you can add 1 to a casting, dispelling or unbinding roll for this general.

6 Cunning: *This devious warlord is kept informed by a vast network of spies.*

After the battle has started, roll a dice each time your opponent receives a command point. On a 6 you receive the command point instead of them.

WARPED INSPIRATIONS
CLANS SKRYRE HERO only.

D6 Command Trait

1 Malevolent: *Spite and hatred drive this warlord to ever greater heights of violence.*

You can re-roll wound rolls of 1 for attacks made with melee weapons by this general.

2 Verminous Valour: *This vicious rat inspires his followers to commit terrible acts of self-sacrifice.*

Before you allocate a wound or mortal wound to this general, you can roll a dice. Subtract 1 from the roll if this general is a **MONSTER** or **WAR MACHINE**. On a 4+, instead of allocating the wound or mortal wound to this general, you can allocate it to a friendly **SKAVENTIDE** unit within 3" of this general.

3 Savage Overlord: *This warlord punishes his minions' transgressions with savage brutality.*

Add 1 to the Bravery characteristic of friendly **SKAVENTIDE** units while they are wholly within 18" of this general.

4 Masterful Scavenger: *This avaricious rat has amassed a great hoard of warpstone sparks.*

Add 2 to the number of warpstone sparks this general's army can use during a battle.

5 Deranged Inventor: *The fell contraptions of this general are unrivalled in their dark genius.*

At the start of your shooting phase, you can pick 1 friendly **CLANS SKRYRE** unit that is wholly within 13" of this general. You can re-roll hit rolls for attacks made with missile weapons by that unit until the end of that phase.

6 Overseer of Destruction: *This general's weapon teams are masters of their deadly trade.*

At the start of your shooting phase, you can pick up to 3 friendly **WEAPON TEAM** units that are wholly within 13" of this general. You can re-roll hit rolls for attacks made by those units until the end of that phase.

CREEDS OF CORRUPTION
Clans Pestilens Hero only.

D6	Command Trait

1   Malevolent: *Spite and hatred drive this warlord to ever greater heights of violence.*

You can re-roll wound rolls of 1 for attacks made with melee weapons by this general.

2   Verminous Valour: *This vicious rat inspires his followers to commit terrible acts of self-sacrifice.*

Before you allocate a wound or mortal wound to this general, you can roll a dice. Subtract 1 from the roll if this general is a **Monster** or **War Machine**. On a 4+, instead of allocating the wound or mortal wound to this general, you can allocate it to a friendly **Skaventide** unit within 3" of this general.

3   Savage Overlord: *This warlord punishes his minions' transgressions with savage brutality.*

Add 1 to the Bravery characteristic of friendly **Skaventide** units while they are wholly within 18" of this general.

4   Master of Rot and Ruin: *This general's presence heralds the coming of the Great Plagues.*

You can re-roll the dice that determines if a prayer chanted by this general is answered.

5   Architect of Death: *A rain of projectile putrescence precedes this general's advance.*

You can re-roll wound rolls for attacks made with missile weapons by friendly **Clans Pestilens** units while they are wholly within 18" of this general.

6   Diseased: *Those who draw too close to this plague-infested rat are consumed by infection.*

At the start of your hero phase, roll a dice if this general is within 3" of any enemy units. On a 4+ inflict D3 mortal wounds on 1 enemy unit within 3" of this general.

TREACHEROUS TACTICS
Clans Verminus Hero only.

D6	Command Trait

1   Malevolent: *Spite and hatred drive this warlord to ever greater heights of violence.*

You can re-roll wound rolls of 1 for attacks made with melee weapons by this general.

2   Verminous Valour: *This vicious rat inspires his followers to commit terrible acts of self-sacrifice.*

Before you allocate a wound or mortal wound to this general, you can roll a dice. Subtract 1 from the roll if this general is a **Monster** or **War Machine**. On a 4+, instead of allocating the wound or mortal wound to this general, you can allocate it to a friendly **Skaventide** unit within 3" of this general.

3   Savage Overlord: *This warlord punishes his minions' transgressions with savage brutality.*

Add 1 to the Bravery characteristic of friendly **Skaventide** units while they are wholly within 18" of this general.

4   Brutal Fury: *In times of greatest need, this general attacks with redoubled fury.*

Once per battle, at the start of the combat phase, you can add 3 to the Attacks characteristic of this general's melee weapons until the end of that phase.

5   Powerful: *This Clawlord is amongst the largest and most powerfully built of his breed.*

Add 1 to this general's Wounds characteristic.

6   Devious Adversary: *This wily skaven knows how best to capitalise on any opening left by his opponent.*

If the unmodified hit roll for an attack made with a melee weapon that targets this general is a 1, add 1 to the Attacks characteristic of this general's melee weapons until the end of that phase.

FLESHMASTERIES
Clans Moulder Hero only.

D6 Command Trait

1 Malevolent: *Spite and hatred drive this warlord to ever greater heights of violence.*

You can re-roll wound rolls of 1 for attacks made with melee weapons by this general.

2 Verminous Valour: *This vicious rat inspires his followers to commit terrible acts of self-sacrifice.*

Before you allocate a wound or mortal wound to this general, you can roll a dice. Subtract 1 from the roll if this general is a **Monster** or **War Machine**. On a 4+, instead of allocating the wound or mortal wound to this general, you can allocate it to a friendly **Skaventide** unit within 3" of this general.

3 Savage Overlord: *This warlord punishes his minions' transgressions with savage brutality.*

Add 1 to the Bravery characteristic of friendly **Skaventide** units while they are wholly within 18" of this general.

4 Moulder Supreme: *The mutated creations of this Master Moulder are beyond compare.*

When you use the Prized Creations battle trait and pick 1 friendly **Clans Moulder Fighting Beast** model for this general, you can either add 3 to that model's Wounds characteristic instead of D3, or add D6 to that model's Wounds characteristic instead of D3.

5 Hordemaster: *The creatures created by this Master Moulder are numberless.*

When this general uses the Unleash More-more Beasts! command ability, you receive a new unit on a roll of 4+ instead of 5+.

6 Burly: *This breeder and mutator is as strong and mean as any of his creations.*

Add 1 to this general's Wounds characteristic.

SHADOWY MASTERIES
Clans Eshin Hero only.

D6 Command Trait

1 Malevolent: *Spite and hatred drive this warlord to ever greater heights of violence.*

You can re-roll wound rolls of 1 for attacks made with melee weapons by this general.

2 Verminous Valour: *This vicious rat inspires his followers to commit terrible acts of self-sacrifice.*

Before you allocate a wound or mortal wound to this general, you can roll a dice. Subtract 1 from the roll if this general is a **Monster** or **War Machine**. On a 4+, instead of allocating the wound or mortal wound to this general, you can allocate it to a friendly **Skaventide** unit within 3" of this general.

3 Savage Overlord: *This warlord punishes his minions' transgressions with savage brutality.*

Add 1 to the Bravery characteristic of friendly **Skaventide** units while they are wholly within 18" of this general.

4 Unrivalled Killer: *Few, if any, can rival this warlord's mastery of the assassin's art.*

You can re-roll hit rolls for attacks made by this general that target the enemy **Hero** chosen for the Masters of Murder battle trait.

5 Shadowmaster: *Not even the most eagle-eyed opponent can spot this stealthy assassin when he hides.*

While this general is within 1" of a terrain feature, this general is not visible to enemy models while they are more than 6" from this general.

6 Incredible Agility: *This skaven moves in leaps and bounds that leave others breathless.*

This general can fly.

ARTEFACTS OF POWER

RELICS OF RUIN
MASTERCLAN HERO only.

D6 Artefact of Power

1 Warpstorm Scroll: *Reading words of power from this tattered scroll, the bearer invokes a sky-splitting storm of lurid green lightning.*

Once per battle, in your hero phase, the bearer can use this scroll. If they do so, roll 1 dice for each enemy unit within 13" of the bearer. On a 4+ that unit suffers D3 mortal wounds.

2 Suspicious Stone: *This orb offers glimpses of those plotting the bearer's demise, though its malicious animus has been known to exaggerate.*

Roll a dice each time you allocate a wound or mortal wound to the bearer. On a 5+ that wound or mortal wound is negated.

3 The Gnawshard: *Said to be a fragment of one of the Horned Rat's fangs, this dagger leaves splinters in the wound that keep chewing until its victim is reduced to a hollow sack of skin.*

Pick 1 of the bearer's melee weapons. If any wounds inflicted by that weapon are allocated to an enemy model and not negated, that enemy model suffers 1 mortal wound at the end of each battle round (even if the wounds inflicted by the Gnawshard are subsequently healed).

4 Skavenbrew: *This foul concoction is brewed from blood and warpstone, and dispensed to expendable underlings to drive them into a short-lived but devastating killing frenzy.*

Once per battle, in your hero phase, you can pick 1 friendly **SKAVENTIDE** unit within 3" of the bearer. That unit suffers D3 mortal wounds, but you can add 1 to the Attacks characteristic of melee weapons used by that unit until your next hero phase.

5 Snoutgrovel Robes: *Soaked in sorcerous treatments refined from the musk of fear, these robes quell the terror of the wearer's underlings.*

Do not take battleshock tests for friendly **SKAVENTIDE** units while they are wholly within 13" of the bearer.

6 Staff of Rightful Supremacy: *This staff radiates oppressive waves of sorcerous energy that smother the inferior magics of the lesser races and can even banish endless spells.*

Subtract 1 from the casting rolls of enemy **WIZARDS** while they are within 13" of the bearer. In addition, once per battle, you can dispel one endless spell within 13" of the caster (you do not have to roll 2D6, the dispel is automatically successful).

DARK INVENTIONS
CLANS SKRYRE HERO only.

D6 Artefact of Power

1 The Brass Orb: *This fist-sized orb of interlocking cogs can tear open the fabric of reality and plunge a nearby foe into the Realm of Chaos.*

Once per battle, at the start of your hero phase, you can roll a dice. On a 6 the closest enemy model within 6" of the bearer is slain. If several enemy models are equally close, you can pick which one is slain.

2 Warpstone Armour: *Wrought from warpstone-infused brass and lined with thaumaconductive wiring, this armour lashes out at those who strike it with arcing blasts of warp lightning.*

Roll a dice each time a wound inflicted by a melee weapon is allocated to the bearer and not negated. On a 5+ the attacking unit suffers 1 mortal wound.

3 Esoteric Warp Resonator: *As each of the thirteen dials on this sealed orb are rotated, the stored warp energy inside causes it to quiver and glow.*

At the start of each battle round you receive 1 extra warpstone spark if the bearer is on the battlefield. That warpstone spark can only be used to perform a warpstone spark ability with the bearer in that battle round. If it is not used before the end of the battle round in which it was received, it is lost.

4 Skryre's-breath Bellows: *Fitted with warpstone-powered turbines, these bellows blow plumes of poisoned wind across friend and foe alike.*

At the start of your hero phase, the bearer can pump the bellows. If they do so, roll a dice for each unit other than the bearer that is within 3" of the bearer. On a 4+ that unit suffers D3 mortal wounds.

5 Vial of the Fulminator: *The highly combustible oil within this vial is the perfect fuel for explosively propelling Skryre war machines across the battlefield.*

At the start of your movement phase, you can pick 1 friendly CLANS SKRYRE WAR MACHINE within 3" of the bearer. Double that unit's Move characteristic until the end of that phase. At the end of that phase, roll a dice. On a 4+ that unit suffers D3 mortal wounds.

6 Vigordust Injector: *The shards of pulverised alchemical agents administered by this syringe cause injected skaven to froth at the mouth as they enter a violent and extremely painful frenzy before dying.*

In your hero phase, you can pick 1 friendly SKAVENTIDE unit wholly within 12" of the bearer. Add 1 to charge rolls and hit rolls for that unit until your next hero phase. However, at the start of your next hero phase that unit suffers D3 mortal wounds.

BEFOULED BOONS
Clans Pestilens Hero only.

D6   Artefact of Power

1 Blade of Corruption: *This rusting blade seethes with a thousand lethal poxes and plagues.*

Pick 1 of the bearer's melee weapons. You can re-roll wound rolls for attacks made with that weapon.

2 The Foul Pendant: *The rank energies that cling to this charm weaken enemy spells just as disease sickens living beings.*

The bearer can attempt to unbind 1 spell in each enemy hero phase in the same manner as a **Wizard**.

3 Brooding Blade: *Those cut by this filthy dagger become host to dozens of plague-bearing rats, who burrow outward through the victim's flesh before spreading disease to those nearby.*

Pick 1 of the bearer's melee weapons. At the end of the combat phase, roll a dice for each model wounded by this weapon but not slain. On a 2+ that model's unit suffers D3 mortal wounds.

4 The Fumigatous: *When a name is spoken while this ornate censer is being swung, the cloud of pungent toxins surrounding it coalesces and seeks out the one who possesses that name.*

At the start of each combat phase, you can pick 1 enemy unit within 6" of the bearer and roll a dice. On a 2+ that unit suffers 1 mortal wound. On a 5+ that unit suffers D3 mortal wounds instead of 1.

5 Blistrevous, the Living Cyst: *This sentient pustule migrates from host to host, whispering its mad ravings to drive its bearer into a fevered frenzy.*

Add 2" to the bearer's Move characteristic. In addition, you can re-roll hit rolls for attacks made by the bearer. Starting from the second battle round, at the start of your hero phase, if there are any other friendly **Clans Pestilens Heroes** within 13" of the bearer, you must transfer this artefact to one of them, even if they already carry an artefact of power.

6 Liber Bubonicus: *This foul book is inscribed with the secrets of every disease in the Mortal Realms.*

The bearer can use the Plague Prayers ability from the Plague Priest warscroll (pg 114). If the bearer is a **Plague Priest**, then it can use the Plague Prayers ability twice in your hero phase.

WARP-TOUCHED WARGEAR
CLANS VERMINUS HERO only.

D6   **Artefact of Power**

1   **Things-Bane:** *This blade has been worked with many foul enchantments to make it anathema to the foes of the skaven. This, of course, is all other races – and even the skaven themselves.*

Pick 1 of the bearer's melee weapons. Add 1 to the Damage characteristic of that weapon.

2   **Shield of Distraction:** *This shield boasts cracked and tilted mirror-surfaces enchanted with unsettling glamours that induce confusion, nausea and paranoia in the foe.*

Re-roll save rolls of 1 for attacks that target the bearer. In addition, at the start of the combat phase, pick 1 enemy model within 3" of the bearer. Subtract 1 from hit rolls for attacks made with melee weapons by that model in that combat phase.

3   **Screechskull Trophies:** *Said to be the trophy rack of a skaven hero from the world-that-was, this elaborate back-banner is festooned with skulls that scream and chatter horrifyingly.*

Subtract 1 from the Bravery characteristic of enemy units while they are within 13" of the bearer.

4   **Flaypelt Cloak:** *This cloak is stitched together from the skins of thirteen slain rivals, whose stolen strength empowers the wearer.*

You can re-roll hit and wound rolls of 1 for attacks made with melee weapons by the bearer.

5   **Rustcursed Armour:** *Not only does this heavy suit of rust-thick armour deflect the blows of the foe, but the ruin-hexes scored into its plates spread tendrils of oxidising entropy across the attacker's most treasured artefacts.*

Re-roll save rolls of 1 for attacks that target the bearer. In addition, at the start of the combat phase, you can pick 1 enemy **HERO** with an artefact of power that is within 3" of the bearer and roll 3D6. If the roll is exactly 13, that artefact of power can no longer be used (if a weapon was picked when the artefact of power was selected, that weapon reverts to normal).

6   **Warpstone Charm:** *This foul talisman radiates waves of mutating energy that reduce the enemy – and eventually the wearer – to heaving heaps of twisted flesh and fur.*

At the start of your hero phase, pick 1 unit within 3" of the bearer and roll a dice. On a 2-5 that unit suffers 1 mortal wound. On a 6 that unit suffers D3 mortal wounds. (Note that if there are no enemy units within 3" you must pick either a friendly unit or the bearer to be the target.)

MONSTROUS ARCANA
Clans Moulder Hero only.

D6   Artefact of Power

1   Lash of Fangs: *This coiling lash is studded with scavenged Jabberslythe fangs. Its bite sends victims into a gibbering spiral of madness.*

Pick 1 of the bearer's melee weapons. If the unmodified hit roll for an attack made with that weapon is 6, that attack inflicts 1 mortal wound on the target in addition to any normal damage.

2   Foulhide: *Fashioned from the flensed flesh of Rat Ogors and soaked in cloying alchemical agents, this stinking armour sticks to its wearer like a bloated second skin and regrows as fast as it can be hacked apart.*

In your hero phase, you can heal up to D3 wounds allocated to the bearer.

3   Snap-snap Snarepole: *This cruelly cursed things-catcher shatters its victims' bones with a crushing noose of magical energy.*

At the start of the combat phase, pick 1 enemy model within 3" of the bearer. Subtract 1 from hit rolls for attacks made by that model in that combat phase.

4   Rat-tail Snake: *A disgusting familiar fashioned from tails, eyes and venomous fangs, this abomination clings to its master's body beneath his ragged robes, and lunges forth to bite any who threaten him.*

If the unmodified save roll for an attack that targets the bearer is 6, the attacking unit suffers 1 mortal wound after all of its attacks have been resolved.

5   Rabid Crown: *This darkly sorcerous nest of electrodes jabs into the wearer's skull and radiates his will, imposing it upon nearby war beasts to drive them into a killing fury.*

You can re-roll wound rolls for attacks made by friendly **Clans Moulder Pack** units while they are wholly within 13" of the bearer.

6   Fleshgift Vial: *Containing the most aggressive fleshmoulding solutions known to the Clans Moulder, when this flask shatters and spills its contents across the enemy they are overcome by immediate and hideous mutative devolution.*

Once per battle, in your shooting phase, you can pick 1 enemy unit within 6" of the bearer and roll a dice. On a 1, the bearer suffers 1 mortal wound. On a 2-5, that enemy unit suffers D3 mortal wounds. On a 6 that enemy unit suffers D6 mortal wounds.

TOOLS OF MURDER
CLANS ESHIN HERO only.

D6 Artefact of Power

1 Shadow Magnet Trinket: *This warpstone-ore pendant absorbs light and engulfs the wearer in an aura of shifting gloom from which they can strike unseen.*

Once per battle, the bearer can fight at the start of the combat phase, before the players pick any other units to fight in that combat phase. The bearer cannot fight again in that combat phase unless an ability or spell allows it to fight more than once.

2 Farskitter Cloak: *With a swirl of this cloak's hem, the wearer can slip through the cracks in reality to squirm back into the light elsewhere.*

Once per battle, at the end of your movement phase, you can remove the bearer from the battlefield and set them up again anywhere on the battlefield more than 9" from any enemy units.

3 The Three Fangs: *Fashioned by blind Eshin artisans from the bones of traitorous triplets, if all three of these blades find their mark in a victim at once, then agonising death is instantaneous.*

Once per battle, at the start of your shooting phase, you can pick 1 enemy **HERO** within 6" of the bearer and roll 3 dice. If all 3 rolls are 3+, and the combined value of the 3 dice is greater than that enemy model's Wounds characteristic, that enemy model is slain.

4 Warpweeper Stars: *So lethal that they must be kept in a lead-lined pouch, these barbed stars have mutating warpstone tips and bleed excruciating acidic venom.*

Pick 1 of the bearer's missile weapons. If the unmodified wound roll for an attack made with that weapon is 6, that attack inflicts D3 mortal wounds on the target in addition to any normal damage.

5 The Cube of Mists: *This ominous puzzle box contains a fragment of Ulguan realmstone. It gives off a constant, eerie fume that distorts perception and tricks the unwary.*

Once per battle, at the start of the combat phase, you can pick 1 enemy unit within 6" of the bearer. That unit cannot make a pile-in move in that combat phase. In addition, subtract 1 from hit rolls for attacks made by that unit in that combat phase.

6 Gnawbomb: *This fearsome weapon uses gnawhole technology to tear a temporary rent in reality.*

Once per battle, in your hero phase, you can pick 1 terrain feature within 6" of the bearer. Until your next hero phase, that terrain feature has the scenery rules from the Gnawhole warscroll (pg 81) in addition to the scenery rules it already has.

SPELL LORES

You can choose or roll for one spell from one of the following tables for each **SKAVEN WIZARD** in a Skaventide army.

LORE OF RUIN
GREY SEER only.

D6 Spell

1 Scorch: *The Grey Seer thrusts out a claw and his foes are roasted alive by a gout of magical flame.*

Scorch has a casting value of 5. If successfully cast, pick 1 enemy unit within 13" of the caster and visible to them, and roll a number of dice equal to the casting roll. For each 6, that unit suffers 1 mortal wound.

2 Splinter: *The Grey Seer gives an atonal shriek that rises in pitch until reality itself shivers, shudders, then cracks asunder.*

Splinter has a casting value of 6. If successfully cast, pick 1 enemy model within 6" of the caster, and roll a dice. If the roll is greater than that model's Wounds characteristic, it is slain.

3 Skitterleap: *The Grey Seer or one of his minions vanishes in a puff of smoke, reappearing elsewhere on the battlefield an eye-blink later.*

Skitterleap has a casting value of 6. If successfully cast, pick 1 friendly **SKAVENTIDE HERO** with a Wounds characteristic of 12 or less, that is within 13" of the caster and visible to them. Remove that **HERO** from the battlefield and then set it up again anywhere on the battlefield more than 9" from any enemy units. That **HERO** may not move in the following movement phase.

4 Plague: *The Grey Seer vomits up the twisted syllables of a dread invocation, unleashing a horrific plague that spreads like wildfire.*

Plague has a casting value of 7. If successfully cast, pick 1 enemy unit within 13" of the caster and roll 1 dice for each model in that unit. For each 5+, that unit suffers 1 mortal wound.

5 Death Frenzy: *With a snarled invocation, the Grey Seer drives its underlings into a froth-jawed murder frenzy.*

Death Frenzy has a casting value of 7. If successfully cast, pick 1 friendly **SKAVENTIDE** unit that is not a **HERO**, which is wholly within 13" of the caster and visible to them. Until your next hero phase, when a model from that unit is slain, before it is removed from play, it can make a pile-in move and then attack with all of the melee weapons it is armed with.

6 Warpgale: *Screeching in an unholy tongue, the Grey Seer parts the veil of reality and draws a ravening gale of unnatural energies forth.*

Warpgale has a casting value of 8. If successfully cast, pick 1 enemy unit within 26" of the caster and visible to them. That unit suffers D3 mortal wounds, and any run or charge rolls for that unit are halved until your next hero phase. If that unit can fly, it cannot fly until your next hero phase (in addition to having its run and charge rolls halved).

LORE OF WARPVOLT GALVANISM
Clans Skryre Wizard only.

D3   **Spell**

1   **More-more-more Warp Power!:** *At great risk, the engineer channels raw warp lightning power to nearby allies or himself, with spectacular pyrotechnic results.*

More-more-more Warp Power! has a casting value of 7. If successfully cast, pick 1 friendly **Clans Skryre** unit wholly within 12" of the caster and visible to them. You can re-roll hit and wound rolls for that unit until your next hero phase. However, at the end of your next hero phase, that unit suffers D3 mortal wounds.

2   **Chain Warp Lightning:** *The warlock hurls a ball of warp lightning that careens across the battlefield striking one target after another.*

Chain Warp Lightning has a casting value of 6. If successfully cast, pick up to D6 different enemy units within 18" of the caster. Each of those units suffers 1 mortal wound.

3   **Warp Lightning Shield:** *The warlock surrounds himself with a protective shield of warp lightning. However, should the shield absorb too much energy, it will overload and explode!*

Warp Lightning Shield has a casting value of 6. If successfully cast, until your next hero phase, the first 3 wounds allocated to the caster in each phase are negated. If a fourth wound is allocated to the caster in the same phase, then the caster suffers D6 mortal wounds and this spell is unbound (the first 3 wounds allocated in that phase are still negated).

GNAWHOLES

A Skaventide army can include up to 3 **GNAWHOLE** terrain features (see opposite). After territories have been chosen but before armies are set up, you can set up the **GNAWHOLES** for your army. Each **GNAWHOLE** must be set up wholly within 8" of the edge of the battlefield, more than 3" from any enemy units or objectives, and more than 1" from any other terrain features. If both players can set up any terrain features before armies are set up, they must roll off, and the winner chooses who sets up their terrain features first.

Morgaz swung his massive choppa, ripping through another skaven neck. The blow sent his victim's head spinning away with a surprised look plastered on its verminous features.

'Keep at 'em ladz!' bellowed Morgaz at the Ironjaw Brutes fighting all around him. 'We's got 'em on da run!'

A ratman clad in black launched itself at him, its extended foot-claw catching him square in the jaw in a vicious flying kick. Roaring, Morgaz swatted his assailant out of the air and stamped on its head. Bone gave way with a satisfying crunch, and Morgaz laughed with the simple exhilaration of battle. Ahead, he saw the last of the skaven were in full and panicked retreat. They scrambled over one another, biting and clawing to reach a great pit full of swirling green energies that pulsed in the ground up ahead. One by one, the skaven flung themselves into the pit, and Morgaz snarled as he realised his quarry were escaping.

'None o' dat ya hairy little gitz!' he roared, and broke into a bullish charge. His Brutes followed him, the ground shaking with their armoured footfalls as they stampeded through the fleeing ratmen. Morgaz grabbed for a skaven but it slipped his grasp, chittering mockingly at him before diving into the pit.

'You ain't gettin' away dat easy,' barked Morgaz, taking a firm grip on his choppa and jumping after the ratman. There was a lurid green flash and he found himself stumbling down a warped tunnel. Perspective wheeled around him, and through a haze of dizziness and nausea Morgaz saw the ratmen vanishing away into the shadows. Yet he found he couldn't pursue, couldn't even take a breath of the swirling green gases that surrounded him.

Morgaz felt his skin tingle, then burn as fell energies assailed him, and to his horror he realised his armour was rusting and his flesh beginning to melt before his eyes. The orruk stumbled a few more paces before his leg-bones snapped like dry tinder and he spilled to the ground with a clatter of disintegrating armour.

'Wha... Mork... kill yooz...' He croaked the words and felt something warm and bubbling spill over his rotting tusks. Furious and bewildered, Morgaz managed one last snarl before his vision turned red then black, and life fled his rotted form.

● SCENERY WARSCROLL ●

GNAWHOLE

Gnawholes split the skin of reality, tearing open like lesions and allowing frenzied skaven swarms to spill forth. Manifesting as whirling green portals, gaping black holes, fume-wreathed chasms and countless other malignant phenomena, these tunnels through reality seep with the ruinous energies of the Horned Rat.

DESCRIPTION
A Gnawhole is a single terrain feature. It is an obstacle.

SCENERY RULES
Tunnels Through Reality: *The skaven can move through gnawholes to invade any corner of the Mortal Realms.*

At the start of your movement phase, you can use 1 **Gnawhole** to transport 1 friendly **Skaventide** unit. In order to do so, that unit must be wholly within 6" of the **Gnawhole**, and a friendly **Skaventide Hero** must be within 6" of the **Gnawhole**.

If this is the case, remove the **Skaventide** unit from the battlefield and then set it up wholly within 6" of another **Gnawhole** and more than 9" from any enemy models. This counts as that unit's move for that movement phase.

Aura of the Horned Rat: *Gnawholes emit unholy radiation that empowers skaven spellcasters but is deadly to other races.*

Skaventide units treat this terrain feature as having the Arcane scenery rule (see right). Other units treat this terrain feature as having the Deadly scenery rule (see right). In addition,

you can add 1 to the dice that determines if a prayer is answered if the prayer is chanted by a friendly **Skaventide Priest** within 1" of a **Gnawhole**.

Arcane: Add 1 to casting and unbinding rolls for **Wizards** while they are within 1" of any Arcane terrain features.

Deadly: Roll a dice for each unit that finishes a normal move or charge move within 1" of any Deadly terrain features. On a 1, that unit suffers D3 mortal wounds.

| KEYWORDS | SCENERY, SKAVENTIDE, GNAWHOLE |

BATTLEPLAN
SKAVENTIDE ASSAULT

It is a time-old tenet of skaven strategy that a fight should never be fair. Thus, when they launch attacks on enemy enclaves and strongholds, the skaven do everything in their power to catch their foes unprepared and unable to defend themselves.

The favoured method for a swarm to assail its enemies is via gnawholes. After all, what resistance can the foe muster when the ratmen emerge suddenly and unexpectedly from yawning rents in the fabric of reality itself? Chittering clawpacks of skaven spill from the swirling shadows of their gnawholes brandishing rusted blades and baring their chisel fangs. Foes reel in shock and confusion as masses of lank-furred killers surge over them, stabbing and biting madly. By the time the enemy truly grasp that they are under attack, the skaven are already victorious.

THE ARMIES
Each player picks an army as described in the core rules. One player is the Skaven player and their opponent is the Defender. The Skaven player must use a Skaventide army.

The Skaventide army has a unique command ability, as follows:

SKAVENTIDE COMMAND ABILITY
Attack-attack!: *With a fearsome screech, the commander of the skaventide orders his minions to advance with all haste.*

The Skaven player can use this command ability at the start of their movement phase. If they do so, they can pick 1 friendly **SKAVENTIDE** unit that arrived from reserve that turn and that is wholly within 18" of their general. That unit can make a normal move in that movement phase.

THE BATTLEFIELD
Set up 2 **GNAWHOLES** in two of the corners of the battlefield and 1 **GNAWHOLE** at the centre of the opposite edge of the battlefield, as shown on the map below. The Skaven player cannot set up any more **GNAWHOLES** in this battle.

SET-UP
The Defender sets up their army first, wholly within their own territory. All of the units in the Skaventide army are set up off the battlefield as reserve units. They must be set up during the battle using the Skaventide Assault rule opposite.

OBJECTIVES
This battle is fought to control one objective. It is located at the centre of the battlefield, as shown on the map.

FIRST TURN
The Skaven player takes the first turn in the first battle round.

SKAVENTIDE ASSAULT

The skaven emerge from their hidden gnawholes, attacking their surprised and disorientated foe from all sides.

At the start of their hero phase, the Skaven player can choose to set up any number of reserve units. The units are set up one at a time, wholly within 9" of a **Gnawhole** and more than 3" from any enemy units. Those units cannot move in the following movement phase, unless the Attack-attack! command ability is used, and the Skaven player cannot use the Tunnels Through Reality scenery rule from the Gnawhole warscroll to transport any unit in the same turn. Any of the Skaven player's reserve units that are not set up on the battlefield before the start of the fourth battle round are destroyed.

TAKEN OFF GUARD

The defenders have absolutely no idea that their once-safe enclave has been chosen as the target for a skaventide assault.

The Defender cannot spend any command points in the first battle round. In addition, the Defender's units cannot run or charge in the first battle round.

GLORIOUS VICTORY

Starting from the third battle round, at the end of each battle round, roll a dice and add the number of the current battle round to the roll. On a 9+ the battle ends. On any other roll, the battle continues.

When the battle ends, the player that controls the objective wins a **major victory**. If neither player controls the objective, both players win a **minor victory**.

BATTLEPLAN
THROUGH THE GNAWHOLE

One of the greatest dangers of facing skaven in battle is that – thanks to their sheer numbers and the anarchic nature of their armies – they often strike from multiple locations at once. At such times, an enemy commander must worry not only about the skaven they can see in front of them, but also those verminous reinforcements that may be flowing in from other battlefields, or even other Mortal Realms. Multiple skaven swarms might even assail an enemy position at the same time not as part of a coordinated offensive, but simply in a competition to prove which skaven leader is superior.

Such dire scenarios are at their most deadly when the skaven manage to link multiple gnawholes to a single exit, allowing them to surge through the void and converge upon their outnumbered enemies in a seething skaventide. The foe can do little but dig in and stand their ground, desperately hoping to weather the skaven assault and hang onto their position until the flood of red-eyed ratmen exhausts itself.

THE ARMIES
Each player picks an army as described in the core rules. One player is the Skaven player and their opponent is the Defender. The Skaven player must use a Skaventide army.

After the players have picked their armies, they must split them into contingents. The Skaventide army has two contingents, and the Defender's army has three contingents. A contingent can have up to 1 more unit than either of the other contingents. For example, if the Defender's army had 10 units, they could split them into two contingents with 3 units and one with 4 units.

THE BATTLEFIELD
This battle is fought across three separate battlefields, each measuring 2' by 4' (see the map below). **Skaventide** units can move from one battlefield to another using the Gnawhole Convergence rule opposite. That aside, units on one battlefield cannot attack, cast spells or use abilities on units that are on a different battlefield. The Skaven player cannot set up any more **Gnawholes** in this battle.

SET-UP
The Defender sets up their army first. They must set up 1 of their army's contingents on each battlefield, wholly within their own territory. The Skaven player sets up their army second. They must set up 1 of their army's contingents wholly within their territory on the left-hand battlefield, and the other wholly within their territory on the right-hand battlefield.

OBJECTIVES
This battle is fought to control one objective. It is located at the centre of the central battlefield, as shown on the map.

FIRST TURN
The Skaven player takes the first turn in the first battle round.

GNAWHOLE CONVERGENCE

The skaven have discovered two different gnawhole tunnels which lead to the same destination.

In this battle, any number of units from the Skaventide army can use the Tunnels Through Reality scenery rule from the Gnawhole warscroll in the same turn. However, the rule can only be used to move units that are on the left-hand and right-hand battlefields to the central battlefield.

HOLD YOUR GROUND!

The core of the defender's forces have been tasked with holding their ground, and preventing the skaven from seizing a vital objective no matter the cost.

Units from the Defender's army that are on the central battlefield cannot move except to make pile-in moves. In addition, do not take battleshock tests for units from the Defender's army that are on the central battlefield.

GLORIOUS VICTORY

Starting from the fourth battle round, if there are no units from the Skaventide army on the central battlefield at the end of a battle round, or if the Skaven player controls the objective, the battle ends.

When the battle ends, the player that controls the objective wins a **major victory**. Any other result is a **draw**.

PATH TO GLORY

Path to Glory campaigns centre around collecting and fighting battles with a warband in the Age of Sigmar. Champions fight each other and gather followers to join them in their quest for glory, taking advantage of this age of unending battle to win glory and renown.

In order to take part in a Path to Glory campaign, you will need two or more players. All players will need to have at least one **Hero**, who is their champion, and must then create a warband to follow and fight beside their champion during the campaign.

The players fight battles against each other using the warbands they have created. The results of these battles will gain their warband favour. The warband will swell in numbers as more warriors flock to their banner, while existing troops become more powerful.

After gaining enough favour or growing your warband enough to dominate all others through sheer weight of numbers, you will be granted a final test. Succeed, and your glory will be affirmed for all time, and you will be crowned as the victor of the campaign.

CREATING A WARBAND
When creating a Path to Glory warband, do not select your army in the normal manner. Instead, your army consists of a mighty champion battling to earn the favour of the gods, and their entire band of loyal followers. As you wage war against other warbands, your own warband will grow, and existing units will become grizzled veterans.

WARBAND ROSTER
The details and progress of each warband need to be recorded on a warband roster, which you can download for free from games-workshop.com.

To create a warband, simply follow these steps and record the results on your warband roster:

1. First, pick an allegiance for your warband. Each allegiance has its own set of warband tables that are used to generate the units in

the warband and the rewards they can receive for fighting battles. The warband tables included in this battletome let you collect a warband with the Skaventide allegiance, but other Warhammer Age of Sigmar publications include warband tables to let you collect other warbands from the Grand Alliances of Order, Chaos, Death and Destruction.

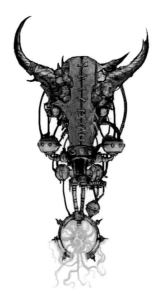

2. Next, choose your warband's champion by selecting one of the options from your allegiance's champion table. The champion you choose will determine the number of followers in your warband. Give your champion a suitably grand name, and write this down on your warband roster.

3. Having picked your champion, the next step is to generate your starting followers. These can be chosen from the followers tables for your allegiance. If your allegiance has more than one followers table you can freely choose which ones you use, selecting all of your followers from a single table or from several. Instead of choosing, you can place

your destiny in the hands of fate and roll on the followers tables instead. To make a followers roll, pick a column from one of the followers tables and then roll a dice.

4. Your followers need to be organised into units. The follower table tells you how many models the unit has. Follower units cannot include additional models, but they can otherwise take any options listed on their warscroll. Record all of the information about your followers on your warband roster.

5. Instead of generating a unit of followers, your champion can start the campaign with a Champion's Reward, or one of your units can start with a Follower's Reward. No champion or unit can start the Path to Glory campaign with more than one reward each.

6. Finally, give your warband a name, one that will inspire respect and dread in your rivals. Your warband is now complete, and you can fight your first battle. Good luck!

TO WAR!
Having created a warband, you can now fight battles with it against other warbands taking part in the campaign. You can fight battles as and when you wish, and can use any of the battleplans available for Warhammer Age of Sigmar.

The units you use for a game must be those on your roster. Units can either be fielded at their full roster strength, or broken down into smaller units, as long as no unit is smaller than the minimum size shown on its pitched battle profile.

Any casualties suffered by a warband are assumed to have been replaced in time for its next battle. If your champion is slain in a battle, it is assumed that they were merely injured, and they are back to full strength for your next game, thirsty for vengeance!

GAINING GLORY

All of the players in the campaign are vying for glory. The amount of glory they have received is represented by the Glory Points that the warband has accumulated. Glory can be increased by fighting and winning battles, as described next. As a warband's glory increases, it will also attract additional followers, and a warband's champion may be granted rewards.

Warbands receive Glory Points after a battle is complete. If the warband drew or lost the battle, it receives 1 Glory Point. If it won the battle, it receives D3 Glory Points (re-roll a result of 1 if it won a major victory).

Add the Glory Points you scored to the total recorded on your roster. Once you have won 10 Glory Points, you will have a chance to win the campaign, as described below.

REWARDS OF BATTLE

Each allegiance has its own set of rewards tables. After each battle you can take one of the three following options. Alternatively, roll a D3 to determine which option to take:

D3 Option

1 **Additional Followers:** More followers flock to your banner. Either select a new unit or roll for a random one from a follower table, then add it to your warband roster. You can choose from any of your own follower tables, or from any of the follower tables from an allied warband table i.e. a warband table whose allegiance is from the same Grand Alliance as your own. In either case, if you wish to add a unit from a follower table that requires more than '1 roll', you must also reduce your Glory Points total by 1 (if you do not have enough Glory Points, you cannot choose a unit from such a table). Once 5 new units have joined your warband, you will have a chance to win the campaign, as described below.

2 **Champion's Reward:** Your champion's prowess grows. Roll on your allegiance's champion rewards table. Note the result on your warband roster. If you roll a result the champion has already received, roll again until you get a different result.

3 **Follower's Reward:** Your warriors become renowned for mighty deeds. Pick a unit of followers (not one from an allied warband table), then roll on your allegiance's followers rewards table. Note the result on your warband roster. If you roll a result the unit has already received, roll again until you get a different result.

ETERNAL GLORY

There are two ways to win a Path to Glory campaign; either by Blood or by Might. To win by Blood your warband must first have 10 Glory Points. To win by Might your warband must have at least 5 additional units of followers. In either case, you must then fight and win one more battle to win the campaign. If the next battle you fight is tied or lost, you do not receive any Glory Points – just keep on fighting battles until you either win the campaign… or another player wins first!

You can shorten or lengthen a campaign by lowering or raising the number of Glory Points needed to win by Blood, or the number of extra units that must join a warband to win by Might. For example, for a shorter campaign, you could say that a warband only needs 5 Glory Points before the final fight, or for a longer one, say that 15 are needed.

SKAVENTIDE WARBAND TABLES

Use the following tables to determine the champion that leads your warband, the followers that make up the units which fight at their side, and the rewards they can receive after battle.

CHAMPION TABLE

Champion	Followers
Verminlord (any type)	2 units
Grey Seer on Screaming Bell	3 units
Plague Priest on Plague Furnace	3 units
Arch-Warlock	4 units
Clawlord	4 units
Deathmaster	4 units
Grey Seer	4 units
Master Moulder	4 units
Plague Priest	4 units
Warlock Bombardier	4 units
Warlock Engineer	4 units

HERO FOLLOWERS TABLE

D6	Followers
1	Clawlord
2	Deathmaster
3	Grey Seer
4	Master Moulder
5	Plague Priest
6	Warlock Bombardier

SKRYRE WEAPONS FOLLOWERS TABLE

D6	Followers
1	1 Doom-Flayer
2	1 Doomwheel
3-4	1 Ratling Gun
5	1 Warpfire Thrower
6	1 Warp-Grinder

RETINUE FOLLOWERS TABLE

D6	Clans Eshin	Clans Moulder	Clans Pestilens	Clans Skryre	Clans Verminus
1-3	10 Night Runners	20 Giant Rats or 4 Rat Swarms	15 Plague Monks	10 Skryre Acolytes	20 Clanrats
4-6	10 Gutter Runners	3 Pack Masters or 2 Rat Ogors	10 Plague Censer Bearers	2 Warplock Jezzails	10 Stormvermin

SPECIAL RETINUE FOLLOWERS TABLE
(uses 2 rolls, or 1 roll and 1 Glory Point)

D6	Clans Moulder	Clans Pestilens	Clans Skryre
1-3	1 Hell Pit Abomination	1 Plagueclaw	1 Warp Lightning Cannon
4-6	1 Hell Pit Abomination	1 Plagueclaw	2 Stormfiends

FOLLOWERS REWARDS TABLE

D6   **Reward**

1   **Children of the Horned Rat:** *Skaven often call upon the Horned Rat to save their lives – sometimes he even listens.*

Once per battle, at the start of any phase, you can declare that this unit is calling on the Horned Rat for protection. If you do so, you can re-roll save rolls for attacks that target this unit until the end of that phase.

2   **Seething Horde:** *These followers are almost countless in number.*

In your hero phase, you can return 1 slain model to this unit. If this unit has a Wounds characteristic of 1, you can return D3 slain models instead of 1. Set up the returning models one at a time within 1" of a model from this unit (this can be a model you returned to the unit earlier in the same phase). Returning models can only be set up within 3" of an enemy unit if one or more models from this unit are already within 3" of that enemy unit.

3   **Hidden Menace:** *These warriors hide in the cracks in reality, springing forth to ambush their foes.*

Instead of setting up this unit on the battlefield, you can place it to one side and say that it is hidden as a reserve unit. If you do so, at the end of your first movement phase, you must set up this unit on the battlefield more than 9" from any enemy units.

4   **Warpstone Fallout:** *These crazed followers of the Horned Rat have consumed prodigious amounts of warpstone.*

In your hero phase, you can roll a dice for each enemy unit within 3" of this unit. On a 6 that enemy unit suffers D3 mortal wounds.

5   **Savage Retreat:** *These warriors are at their most dangerous when they flee for their lives.*

If this unit fails a battleshock test, you can pick 1 enemy unit within 3" of this unit and roll a dice. On a 4+ that enemy unit suffers 1 mortal wound for each model from this unit that flees.

6   **Scrabbling Tide:** *This clawpack pours towards the foe, clambering over their comrades in order to attack.*

All of this unit's melee weapons are treated as having a range of 3".

CHAMPION REWARDS TABLE

2D6   **Reward**

2   **Punished for Incompetence:** *The Horned Rat does not suffer fools or ineffectual underlings gladly.*

You lose 1 Glory Point. In addition, your champion cannot gain any further rewards for the rest of the campaign.

3   **Scabrous:** *This mangy creature is so scrofulous and diseased that few dare approach too closely.*

Subtract 1 from hit rolls for attacks made with melee weapons that target your champion.

4   **Flurry of Blows:** *When cornered, this crazed follower of the Horned Rat attacks with redoubled fury.*

Once per battle, when your champion attacks, can say that your champion is making a flurry of blows. If you do so, double the Attacks characteristic of any melee weapons used by your champion until the end of that phase.

5   **Malevolent:** *Spite and hatred drive this warlord to ever greater heights of violence.*

You can re-roll wound rolls of 1 for attacks made with melee weapons by your champion.

6   **Verminous Valour:** *This vicious rat inspires his followers to commit terrible acts of self-sacrifice.*

Before you allocate a wound or mortal wound to your champion, you can roll a dice. Subtract 1 from the roll if your champion is a **MONSTER** or **WAR MACHINE**. On a 4+, instead of allocating the wound or mortal wound to your champion, you can allocate it to a unit from the same warband within 3" of your champion.

7   **Survivor:** *One way or another, this resourceful champion always finds a way to get out of danger.*

You can re-roll save rolls for attacks that target your champion.

8   **Savage Overlord:** *This warlord punishes his minions' transgressions with savage brutality.*

Add 1 to the Bravery characteristic of units from your warband while they are wholly within 18" of your champion.

9   **Warpstone Weapon:** *Weapons crafted from warpstone are prized for their extreme lethality.*

Pick 1 of your champion's melee weapons and note it down on your warband roster as being made of warpstone. Add 1 to that weapon's Damage characteristic.

10   **Nefarious:** *This cunning schemer is able to turn even a minor victory into a masterful example of his own prowess.*

Add 1 to the Glory Points you earn if you win a battle and your champion was in your warband.

11   **Protection of the Horned Rat:** *An eerie sense of watchfulness surrounds this champion, and an unholy aura of warding protects him from harm.*

Roll a dice each time you allocate a wound or mortal wound to this champion. On a 5+ that wound or mortal wound is negated.

12   **Rewarded for Excellence:** *The Horned Rat sends forth one of his minions to aid the champion in a vital battle.*

Once during the campaign, you can include 1 **VERMINLORD** in your warband, in addition to any other models you can take.

Amidst the ruins of a fallen magmahold, skaven and Fyreslayers do battle for ancient treasures.

WARSCROLLS

This section includes Skaventide warscrolls, warscroll battalions and endless spell warscrolls. Updated February 2019; the warscrolls printed here take precedence over any warscrolls with an earlier publication date or no publication date.

WARSCROLL BATTALION

VIRULENT PROCESSION

Massed around the looming horror of a Verminlord Corruptor, the Plague Monks of a Virulent Procession surge into battle with maddened shrieks to hack, bite and infect all before them. As diseased corpsemeat piles up across the killing ground, plague-ridden rats boil up from the shadows to feast upon the living and the dead alike.

ORGANISATION

A Virulent Procession consists of the following units and warscroll battalions:

- 1 Verminlord Corruptor

- 2+ Congregations of Filth

- 0-1 Foulrain Congregation

- 0-1 Plaguesmog Congregation

ABILITIES

Verminous Infestation: *As the Virulent Procession advances, plague rats surge forth in furry waves from their hiding places to gnaw upon and infect the enemies of the Horned Rat.*

At the start of your hero phase, pick 1 terrain feature within 13" of this battalion's **VERMINLORD CORRUPTOR**. Roll a dice for each enemy unit within 3" of that terrain feature. On a 4+ that unit suffers D3 mortal wounds.

WARSCROLL BATTALION
CONGREGATION OF FILTH

ORGANISATION

A Congregation of Filth consists of the following units:

- 1 Plague Priest on Plague Furnace

- 2+ units of Plague Monks

ABILITIES

Plague Altar: *The Plague Monks that accompany a Plague Furnace will fight to their last breath for the greater glory of the Horned Rat.*

Roll a dice each time you allocate a wound or mortal wound to a **PLAGUE MONKS** unit from this battalion while it is wholly within 18" of the same battalion's **PLAGUE PRIEST**. On a 6 that wound or mortal wound is negated.

WARSCROLL BATTALION
FOULRAIN CONGREGATION

ORGANISATION

A Foulrain Congregation consists of the following units:

- 1 Plague Priest

- 3 Plagueclaws

ABILITIES

Foetid Blessings: *The Plague Priest of a Foulrain Congregation infuses the vile ammunition of his followers' Plagueclaws with especially virulent diseases.*

Add 1 to wound rolls for attacks made with missile weapons by units in this battalion while they are within 13" of the same battalion's **PLAGUE PRIEST**.

WARSCROLL BATTALION
PLAGUESMOG CONGREGATION

ORGANISATION

A Plaguesmog Congregation consists of the following units:

- 1 Plague Priest on Plague Furnace

- 2+ units of Plague Censer Bearers

ABILITIES

Poisonous Miasma: *So thick is the roiling cloud of poisonous smoke that issues from a Plaguesmog Congregation that to breathe its tainted air is a death sentence.*

You can re-roll the dice that determines if an enemy unit suffers any mortal wounds when you use the Poisonous Fumes ability if that enemy unit is within 3" of a unit from this battalion.

WARSCROLL BATTALION
WARPCOG CONVOCATION

The Warpcog Convocations of the Clans Skryre go to war amid the hiss, whirr, clatter and roar of their many unstable yet deadly war machines. From hails of bullets to blasts of flame, they unleash myriad forms of death upon the shrieked orders of their ruling Arch-Warlocks.

ORGANISATION

A Warpcog Convocation consists of the following units and Enginecovens:

- 1 Arch-Warlock

- 2-5 Enginecovens chosen in any combination from the following list:

  - *Arkhspark Voltik:* 1 Warlock Engineer or Warlock Bombardier, 1-3 Warp Lightning Cannons

  - *Gautfyre Skorch:* 1 Warlock Engineer or Warlock Bombardier, 1-4 units of Stormfiends, 1-5 Warpfire Throwers, 1-5 Warp Grinders

- *Gascloud Chokelung:* 1 Warlock Engineer or Warlock Bombardier, 1-3 units of Stormfiends, 2-5 units of Skryre Acolytes

- *Rattlegauge Warplock:* 1 Warlock Engineer or Warlock Bombardier, 1-3 units of Stormfiends, 1-3 units of Warplock Jezzails, 1-5 Ratling Guns

- *Whyrlblade Threshik:* 1 Warlock Engineer or Warlock Bombardier, 1-3 units of Stormfiends, 1-3 Doomwheels, 1-5 Doom-Flayers

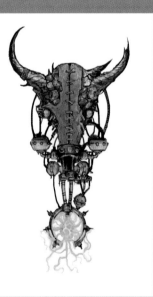

ABILITIES

Arkhspark Voltik: *This enginecoven's warlock fine-tunes the energy output of its Warp Lightning Cannons.*

In your shooting phase, you can pick 1 **WARP LIGHTNING CANNON** from this enginecoven that is within 13" of the **WARLOCK ENGINEER** from the same enginecoven, or the **ARCH-WARLOCK** from the same battalion. If you do so, subtract 1 from the power of that **WARP LIGHTNING CANNON**'s Warp Lightning Blast in that shooting phase (to a minimum power of 1).

Gascloud Chokelung: *The warlock of this enginecoven makes sure that none of his minions waste their precious poisoned wind globes.*

You can re-roll hit rolls of 1 for attacks made with missile weapons by this enginecoven's **SKRYRE ACOLYTES** and **STORMFIENDS** armed with Windlaunchers while they are wholly within 13" of the **WARLOCK ENGINEER** from the same enginecoven, or the **ARCH-WARLOCK** from the same battalion.

Gautfyre Skorch: *The crews of this enginecoven's Warp-Grinders are forced by their warlock to build especially large and elaborate tunnel networks.*

Up to 2 units can join each **WARP-GRINDER** from this enginecoven instead of only 1, as long as both of the units come from the same enginecoven as the **WARP-GRINDER** that they join tunnelling.

Rattlegauge Warplock: *This enginecoven's warlock makes his minions practise constantly to improve their aim.*

You can re-roll hit rolls of 1 for attacks made with missile weapons by this enginecoven's **WARPLOCK JEZZAILS** and **RATLING GUNS** while they are wholly within 13" of the **WARLOCK ENGINEER** from the same enginecoven, or the **ARCH-WARLOCK** from the same battalion.

Whyrlblade Threshik: *This enginecoven's overseer drives his minions forward relentlessly.*

You can move a unit from this enginecoven an extra 3" when it starts the move wholly within 13" of the **WARLOCK ENGINEER** from the same enginecoven, or the **ARCH-WARLOCK** from the same battalion.

Tydaeus Foebreaker stared out into the dawn mists. Behind the sigmarite faceplate of his helm, the Stormcast Eternal's eyes were narrowed. He could feel the taint of Chaos somewhere out there, concealed amidst the dense fog, growing closer by the moment. He glanced left and right. Several dozen Celestial Knights waited along the line of the ancient, moss-thick wall, Judicators at vantage points with their skybolt bows ready, Liberators and Retributors anchoring the gaps in the age-old fortification.

Let the enemy come, thought Tydaeus. The servants of Sigmar were prepared.

He didn't have long to wait. From the mists, Tydaeus heard the grind of metal on metal, interspersed with a harsh crackling and the rumbling roar of mechanical engines. Green light flashed and leapt. Weird sounds multiplied and drew closer by the moment – scrabbling talons, clinking and clattering, loud thuds and gassy roars.

When the first shots came, they were so sudden that even the Stormcasts were caught by surprise. Green streaks cut the air, leaving swirling tunnels of mist in their wake. By the time he heard the crack of weapons discharge, several Judicators had already been smashed backwards from their vantage points to crash down with glowing craters blasted through their armour. Lightning flared as their souls broke free from their bodies and shot to the skies. Tydaeus would see those comrades beyond the anvils, he thought, but for now the living must fight on.

His keen eyes caught tumbling movement above, objects plunging down upon the Stormcast lines.

'Projectiles incoming!' he bellowed, hurling himself sideways as a spinning glass globe bigger than his head smashed down where he had stood. It shattered, noxious green fumes boiling from inside and blistering the grass black where they touched. Several of his comrades were not so fortunate, sigmarite rusting and flesh sloughing away as the poisoned wind did its work. More souls flashed heavenwards, and Tydaeus snarled his anger.

At last the mists began to tatter apart, shredded and scattered by the rising winds, and as they did, Tydaeus beheld the enemy proper. Dozens of arcane war engines churned forward on huge iron-banded wheels. Lumbering rat-monsters stomped closer, their swollen bodies plated in armour, their limbs ending in lethal-looking firearms and combat weapons. Two-skaven teams lugged strange contraptions into battle, and as they squeezed their triggers they unleashed hails of shots and roaring columns of green-black flame into the Stormcast lines.

'Forward, brothers and sisters, slay the tainted vermin!' bellowed Tydaeus, yet even as he broke into a heroic charge, he knew his comrades could not prevail.

WARSCROLL BATTALION
CLAW-HORDE

Personally selected by a Clawlord to serve as his enforcers and living shields, the ratmen of the Claw-hordes fight with particular ferocity, for they know that success in their master's sight may bring the chance of reward, advancement, and perhaps even a chance to supplant him. Failure, on the other hand, is met only with death.

ORGANISATION

A Claw-horde consists of the following units:

- 1 Clawlord
- 1-3 units of Stormvermin
- 2-9 units of Clanrats

ABILITIES

Claw-picked: *The Stormvermin and Clanrats in a Verminus Claw-horde are carefully selected by its Clawlord for their aggression and cunning.*

When the **CLAWLORD** from this battalion use the Gnash-gnaw on their Bones! command ability, instead of picking 1 unit wholly within 13" of the **CLAWLORD**, you can pick all of the units from the same battalion that are wholly within 13" of the **CLAWLORD**.

WARSCROLL BATTALION
FLESHMELD MENAGERIE

When a Master Moulder gathers the full might of his underlings and beast packs about him, such formations are known as Fleshmeld Menageries. They take the form of wave upon wave of twisted abominations, verminous terrors both large and small that scramble over and around one another in order to sink their fangs into the foe.

ORGANISATION

A Fleshmeld Menagerie consists of the following units:

- 1 Master Moulder

- 0-3 Hell Pit Abominations

- 1-3 units of Packmasters

- 1-4 units of Rat Swarms or Giant Rats in any combination

- 1-4 units of Rat Ogors

ABILITIES

More-more-more Beasts!: *The Master Moulder that commands a Fleshmeld Menagerie has created an almost endless horde of beasts.*

When the Master Moulder from this battalion uses the Unleash More-more Beasts! command ability for a unit from the same battalion that has been destroyed, a new unit is added to your army on a roll of 4+ instead of 5+.

WARSCROLL BATTALION
SLINKTALON

A Slinktalon is an assassination force of Eshin operatives led by a devious Deathmaster, which closes like a noose of shadow around its victims. Only when they are perfectly poised do the skaven strike as one, taking their cue from their master and hitting their targets from all sides in a blizzard of throwing stars and envenomed blades.

ORGANISATION

A Slinktalon consists of the following units:

- 1 Deathmaster
- 1-4 units of Gutter Runners
- 2-8 units of Night Runners

ABILITIES

Murder-slay, Now-now!: *At the Deathmaster's command, the Slinktalon executes its carefully conceived assassination plan.*

If the **DEATHMASTER** from this battalion is set up in hiding as a reserve unit, in the combat phase in which it is set up on the battlefield you can re-roll hit rolls for attacks made by units from the same battalion.

THANQUOL
ON BONERIPPER

MOVE *
WOUNDS 14
SAVE 4+
BRAVERY 7

Grey Seer Thanquol is a paranoid megalomaniac with a warpstone addiction and a brain full of fevered schemes for greatness. Riding on the shoulders of his monstrous Rat Ogor, Boneripper, he unleashes sorcerous fury on all who stand in his way.

MISSILE WEAPONS	Range	Attacks	To Hit	To Wound	Rend	Damage
Warpfire Projectors	8"			See below		
MELEE WEAPONS	**Range**	**Attacks**	**To Hit**	**To Wound**	**Rend**	**Damage**
Staff of the Horned Rat	2"	2	4+	3+	-1	D3
Warpfire Braziers	2"	See below	3+	3+	-2	3
Crushing Blows	2"	*	4+	3+	-1	2

DAMAGE TABLE			
Wounds Suffered	Move	Crushing Blows	Staff of the Horned Rat
0-3	10"	6	+2
4-5	9"	5	+2
6-8	8"	4	+1
9-10	7"	3	+1
11+	6"	2	0

DESCRIPTION

Thanquol on Boneripper is a named character that is a single model. He is armed with the Staff of the Horned Rat.

MOUNT: Thanquol's mount, Boneripper, is armed with a total of four warpfire weapons, which can be any combination of Warpfire Braziers and/or Warpfire Projectors.

ABILITIES

Protection of the Horned Rat: *Thanquol has had more than his fair share of miraculous escapes. He attributes these to his own genius and wondrous good fortune, but in truth the Great Horned Rat keeps one eye on his antics and – on occasion – indulgently wards him from harm.*

Roll a dice each time you allocate a wound or mortal wound to this model. On a 5+ that wound or mortal wound is negated.

Staff of the Horned Rat: *Thanquol can draw on the magical energy stored in his staff to enhance the spells that he casts. Once, he viewed this as the blessings of the Horned One made manifest; now, he sees it simply as cunningly acquired power.*

Add the Staff of the Horned Rat modifier shown on the damage table above to casting rolls for this model.

Warp-amulet: *Thanquol wears a thrumming green warpstone amulet, the mutating magics of which serve to meld and rapidly heal his or Boneripper's flesh if either of them is injured.*

In your hero phase, you can heal 1 wound allocated to this model.

Warpfire Braziers: *These enormous, fume-belching wrecking balls allow Boneripper to crush the largest foes with ease.*

The Attacks characteristic for this model's Warpfire Braziers is equal to double the number of Warpfire Braziers that Boneripper is armed with.

Warpfire Projectors: *These horrific weapons engulf the target in searing gouts of warpfire.*

Do not use the attack sequence for an attack made with Warpfire Projectors. Instead, roll X dice for each model in the target unit that is within 8" of this model, where X is equal to the number of Warpfire Projectors this model is armed with. For each 4+ the target unit suffers 1 mortal wound.

Warpstone Addiction: *Thanquol is addicted to warpstone, and can consume it in quantities that would kill any other Grey Seer. This serves to supercharge his magics, though not without eroding his sanity and ravaging his scrawny frame.*

Once in each of your hero phases, when this model attempts to cast a spell, you can say it will consume a warpstone token before you make the casting roll. If you do so, roll 3D6. This roll cannot be re-rolled or modified. If the 3D6 roll is 13, the spell is cast and cannot be unbound, and after the effects of the spell have been resolved this model suffers D6 mortal wounds. If the 3D6 roll was not 13, remove 1 dice of your choice, and then use the remaining 2D6 as the casting roll.

MAGIC

Thanquol on Boneripper is a **WIZARD**. He can attempt to cast two spells in your hero phase, and attempt to unbind two spells in the enemy hero phase. He knows the Arcane Bolt, Mystic Shield and Madness spells.

Madness: *Thanquol twists the perception of a nearby foe so that they lash out at everyone around them, or even attack themselves.*

Madness has a casting value of 8. If successfully cast, pick 1 enemy **HERO** within 3" of the caster and visible to them, and roll a number of dice equal to the combined value of the Attacks characteristics of all melee weapons that **HERO** is armed with. For each 5+ you can inflict 1 mortal wound on 1 enemy unit within 3" of that **HERO** (you can choose different units to suffer the mortal wounds if you wish).

COMMAND ABILITIES

Power Behind the Throne: *Thanquol manipulates all around him, letting others think they are in charge when in fact they are only carrying out his wishes.*

You can use this command ability at the start of your hero phase. If you do so, until your next hero phase, one friendly **SKAVEN HERO** other than this model can use the At the Double command ability without a command point being spent; another friendly **SKAVEN HERO** other than this model can use the Forward to Victory command ability without a command point being spent; and a third friendly **SKAVEN HERO** other than this model can use the Inspiring Presence command ability without a command point being spent.

KEYWORDS	CHAOS, SKAVEN, SKAVENTIDE, MASTERCLAN, MONSTER, HERO, WIZARD, GREY SEER, THANQUOL

LORD SKREECH VERMINKING

MOVE 12
WOUNDS 10
SAVE 4+
BRAVERY 100

Malevolent and terrifying beyond words, this most ancient and monstrous of all the Verminlords is a blight upon reality. He can draw upon the masteries of all his anarchic species, and wields the most dire sorceries in all skavendom.

MISSILE WEAPONS	Range	Attacks	To Hit	To Wound	Rend	Damage
Prehensile Tails	6"	✷	3+	3+	-1	1
MELEE WEAPONS	**Range**	**Attacks**	**To Hit**	**To Wound**	**Rend**	**Damage**
Doom Glaive	3"	6	3+	3+	-1	D3
Plaguereaper	1"	✷	3+	3+	-1	1

DAMAGE TABLE			
Wounds Suffered	Move	Prehensile Tails	Plaguereaper
0-2	12"	4	8
3-4	10"	3	7
5-7	8"	2	6
8-9	6"	1	5
10+	4"	0	4

DESCRIPTION

Lord Skreech Verminking is a named character that is a single model. He is armed with a Doom Glaive, a Plaguereaper and Prehensile Tails.

ABILITIES

Protection of the Horned Rat: *An eerie sense of watchfulness surrounds this being, and an unholy aura of warding protects them from harm.*

Roll a dice each time you allocate a wound or mortal wound to this model. On a 5+ that wound or mortal wound is negated.

Terrifying: *This horrific monstrosity strikes fear deep into the hearts of its enemies.*

Subtract 1 from the Bravery characteristic of enemy units while they are within 3" of any models with this ability.

The Thirteen-headed One: *Lord Verminking can call upon his knowledge of the shadowslinking of Eshin, the fleshcrafting of Moulder, the plague-brewing of Pestilens, the warp-tech of Skryre, the warrior skill of Verminus or the arcane lore of the Masterclan.*

At the start of your hero phase, pick 1 one of the following areas of knowledge for this model to draw upon. The rule for that area of knowledge applies to this model until your next hero phase. You cannot pick the same area of knowledge more than once per battle.

Knowledge of the Arcane: Add 1 to casting, dispelling and unbinding rolls for this model.

Knowledge of Fleshcrafting: Heal D3 wounds allocated to this model when you pick this area of knowledge.

Knowledge of Plague-brewing: If the unmodified hit roll for an attack made with this model's Plaguereaper is 6, that attack inflicts 1 mortal wound on the target in addition to any normal damage.

Knowledge of Shadowslinking: Subtract 1 from hit rolls for attacks that target this model.

Knowledge of Warp-tech: This model's Doom Glaive has a Rend characteristic of -3 instead of -1.

Knowledge of the Warrior: Add 1 to hit rolls for attacks made by this model.

MAGIC

Lord Skreech Verminking is a **WIZARD**. He can attempt to cast two spells in your hero phase, and attempt to unbind two spells in the enemy hero phase. He knows the Arcane Bolt, Mystic Shield and Dreaded Thirteenth Spell spells.

Dreaded Thirteenth Spell: *With a sickening lurch, the fabric of reality is torn open by the twisting, mutating power of the Great Horned Rat.*

The Dreaded Thirteenth Spell has a casting value of 8. If successfully cast, pick 1 enemy unit within 13" of the caster and visible to them, and roll 13 dice. For each 4+ that unit suffers 1 mortal wound. You can then summon 1 unit of **CLANRATS** to the battlefield, and add it to your army. The summoned unit can have up to 1 model for each mortal wound that was inflicted by this spell. The summoned unit must be set up wholly within 13" of the caster and more than 9" from any enemy units. The summoned unit cannot move in the following movement phase.

COMMAND ABILITIES

The Rat King: *The warriors of the skaventides fight with rabid fury at Lord Skreech's command, in a futile attempt to curry his favour.*

You can use this command ability at the start of the combat phase. If you do so, in that phase you can re-roll wound rolls of 1 for attacks made by friendly **SKAVENTIDE** units while they are wholly within 13" of a friendly model with this command ability.

KEYWORDS	CHAOS, DAEMON, VERMINLORD, SKAVENTIDE, MASTERCLAN, MONSTER, HERO, WIZARD, LORD SKREECH VERMINKING

VERMINLORD DECEIVER

Abominations shrouded in darkness and dread, Verminlord Deceivers move like lightning and strike like death's own blade. Leaping through the ether, they burst from the shadows in a whirlwind of murder before vanishing without trace.

MISSILE WEAPONS	Range	Attacks	To Hit	To Wound	Rend	Damage
Doomstar	13"	1	3+	3+	-1	D3
Prehensile Tails	6"	✹	3+	3+	-1	1
MELEE WEAPONS	Range	Attacks	To Hit	To Wound	Rend	Damage
Warpstiletto	1"	6	3+	✹	-3	D3

DAMAGE TABLE			
Wounds Suffered	Move	Prehensile Tails	Warpstiletto
0-2	12"	4	2+
3-4	10"	3	3+
5-7	8"	2	3+
8-9	6"	1	4+
10+	4"	0	4+

DESCRIPTION

A Verminlord Deceiver is a single model armed with a Warpstiletto, Doomstar and Prehensile Tails.

ABILITIES

Doomstar: *A Doomstar is a triple-bladed throwing star of horrific size whose blades are sharp enough to cut reality itself. When hurled, it scythes down foes in a great circling arc before returning to the Verminlord's waiting claws.*

A Doomstar has a Damage characteristic of D6 instead of D3 if the target unit has 10 or more models.

Protection of the Horned Rat: *An eerie sense of watchfulness surrounds this being, and an unholy aura of warding protects them from harm.*

Roll a dice each time you allocate a wound or mortal wound to this model. On a 5+ that wound or mortal wound is negated.

Shrouded In Darkness: *Verminlord Deceivers are wreathed in shifting veils of unnatural shadow that obscure their monstrous forms.*

Subtract 2 from hit rolls for attacks made with missile weapons that target this model.

Terrifying: *This horrific monstrosity strikes fear deep into the hearts of its enemies.*

Subtract 1 from the Bravery characteristic of enemy units while they are within 3" of any models with this ability.

MAGIC

This model is a **WIZARD**. It can attempt to cast two spells in your hero phase, and attempt to unbind two spells in the enemy hero phase. It knows the Arcane Bolt, Mystic Shield and Dreaded Skitterleap spells.

Dreaded Skitterleap: *The Verminlord Deceiver or one of his minions vanishes in a puff of smoke, only to reappear elsewhere on the battlefield an eye-blink later.*

Dreaded Skitterleap has a casting value of 6. If successfully cast, pick 1 friendly **SKAVENTIDE HERO** with a Wounds characteristic of 12 or less that is within 26" of the caster and visible to them. Remove that **HERO** from the battlefield and then set it up again anywhere on the battlefield more than 6" from any enemy units. That **HERO** may not move in the following movement phase.

COMMAND ABILITIES

Lord of Assassins: *The skulking warriors of the Clans Eshin will attack viciously at the command of a Verminlord Deceiver.*

You can use this command ability in your shooting phase or any combat phase. If you do so, pick 1 friendly model with this command ability. In that phase, you can re-roll wound rolls for friendly **CLANS ESHIN** units while they are wholly within 13" of that model.

KEYWORDS	CHAOS, DAEMON, VERMINLORD, SKAVENTIDE, CLANS ESHIN, MONSTER, HERO, WIZARD, VERMINLORD DECEIVER

MOVE	WOUNDS	SAVE	BRAVERY
12		4+	10

VERMINLORD CORRUPTOR

Ancient and malevolent, this eldritch servant of the Horned Rat is corruption personified, and a single hissed syllable or flick of its sickle-blades can reduce the mightiest foes to a heap of putrid ooze in seconds.

MISSILE WEAPONS	Range	Attacks	To Hit	To Wound	Rend	Damage
Prehensile Tails	6"	✸	3+	3+	-1	1
MELEE WEAPONS	**Range**	**Attacks**	**To Hit**	**To Wound**	**Rend**	**Damage**
Plaguereapers	1"	✸	3+	3+	-	1

DAMAGE TABLE			
Wounds Suffered	Move	Prehensile Tails	Plaguereapers
0-2	12"	4	10
3-4	10"	3	9
5-7	8"	2	8
8-9	6"	1	7
10+	4"	0	6

DESCRIPTION

A Verminlord Corruptor is a single model armed with Plaguereapers and Prehensile Tails.

ABILITIES

Plaguereapers: *These sickle-like blades drip with the accumulated filth of a thousand diseased middens. The slightest nick or cut from them poisons the blood and reduces flesh to sloughing slime.*

If the unmodified hit roll for an attack made with this model's Plaguereapers is 6, that attack inflicts 1 mortal wound and the attack sequence ends (do not make a wound or save roll).

Plaguemaster: *A Verminlord Corruptor is utterly infested with hideous parasites that spill forth to bedevil its foes, even as its unholy miasma curdles their breath in their lungs and rots their bones from within.*

At the end of the combat phase, roll 1 dice for each enemy unit within 1" of this model. On a 4+ that enemy unit suffers D3 mortal wounds.

Protection of the Horned Rat: *An eerie sense of watchfulness surrounds this being, and an unholy aura of warding protects them from harm.*

Roll a dice each time you allocate a wound or mortal wound to this model. On a 5+ that wound or mortal wound is negated.

Terrifying: *This horrific monstrosity strikes fear deep into the hearts of its enemies.*

Subtract 1 from the Bravery characteristic of enemy units while they are within 3" of any models with this ability.

MAGIC

This model is a **WIZARD**. It can attempt to cast two spells in your hero phase, and attempt to unbind two spells in the enemy hero phase. It knows the Arcane Bolt, Mystic Shield and Dreaded Plague spells.

Dreaded Plague: *The Verminlord Corruptor vomits up the twisted syllables of a dread invocation, unleashing a horrific ensorcelled plague that spreads like wildfire through the enemy ranks and rapidly reduces its victims to split and seeping corpses.*

Dreaded Plague has a casting value of 7. If successfully cast, pick 1 enemy unit within 13" of the caster and roll 1 dice for each model in that unit. For each 4+ that unit suffers 1 mortal wound.

COMMAND ABILITIES

Lord of Pestilence: *The diseased warriors of the Clans Pestilens are driven into an even greater frenzy by the commands of a Verminlord Corruptor.*

You can use this command ability in the combat phase. If you do so, pick 1 friendly model with this command ability. In that phase, you can re-roll hit rolls for friendly **CLANS PESTILENS** units while they are wholly within 13" of that model.

KEYWORDS	CHAOS, DAEMON, VERMINLORD, SKAVENTIDE, NURGLE, CLANS PESTILENS, MONSTER, HERO, WIZARD, VERMINLORD CORRUPTOR

VERMINLORD WARBRINGER

MOVE ✦
WOUNDS 12
SAVE 4+
BRAVERY 10

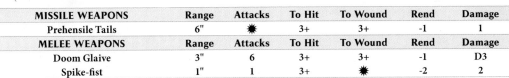

Verminlord Warbringers are toweringly arrogant monstrosities whose every instinct screams for conquest at any price, and whose martial skill is preternatural. None can long stand against them before being reduced to gory trophies.

MISSILE WEAPONS	Range	Attacks	To Hit	To Wound	Rend	Damage
Prehensile Tails	6"	✦	3+	3+	-1	1
MELEE WEAPONS	**Range**	**Attacks**	**To Hit**	**To Wound**	**Rend**	**Damage**
Doom Glaive	3"	6	3+	3+	-1	D3
Spike-fist	1"	1	3+	✦	-2	2

DAMAGE TABLE			
Wounds Suffered	Move	Prehensile Tails	Spike-fist
0-2	12"	4	2+
3-4	10"	3	3+
5-7	8"	2	3+
8-9	6"	1	4+
10+	4"	0	4+

DESCRIPTION

A Verminlord Warbringer is a single model armed with a Doom Glaive, Spike-fist and Prehensile Tails.

ABILITIES

Amidst the Seething Tide: *Warbringers draw strength from being immersed in a scrabbling tide of Verminus worshippers.*

You can re-roll wound rolls for attacks made by this model while it is within 13" of 13 or more friendly **SKAVEN** models.

Fist of Verminus Supremacy: *Warbringers drive their spike-fists into their enemy's weak spots, exploiting the slightest gap in their foe's defences to deliver a bloody coup de grace.*

If the unmodified wound roll for an attack made with this model's Spike-fist is 6, add 4 to the damage inflicted by that attack.

Protection of the Horned Rat: *An eerie sense of watchfulness surrounds this being, and an unholy aura of warding protects them from harm.*

Roll a dice each time you allocate a wound or mortal wound to this model. On a 5+ that wound or mortal wound is negated.

Terrifying: *This horrific monstrosity strikes fear deep into the hearts of its enemies.*

Subtract 1 from the Bravery characteristic of enemy units while they are within 3" of any models with this ability.

MAGIC

This model is a **WIZARD**. It can attempt to cast two spells in your hero phase, and attempt to unbind two spells in the enemy hero phase. It knows the Arcane Bolt, Mystic Shield and Dreaded Death Frenzy spells.

Dreaded Death Frenzy: *With a snarled invocation of goading, the Warbringer triggers the black hunger in its underlings, driving them into a froth-jawed murder frenzy.*

Dreaded Death Frenzy has a casting value of 7. If successfully cast, pick up to D3 friendly **SKAVENTIDE** units wholly within 13" of the caster and visible to them. Until your next hero phase, when a model from any of those units is slain, before it is removed from play, it can make a pile-in move and then attack with all of the melee weapons it is armed with.

COMMAND ABILITIES

Tyrant of Battle: *The fierce warriors of the Clans Verminus will attack with terrible vigour at the command of a Verminlord Warbringer.*

You can use this command ability in the combat phase. If you do so, pick 1 friendly model with this command ability. In that phase, you can re-roll hit and wound rolls of 1 for friendly **CLANS VERMINUS** units while they are wholly within 13" of that model.

KEYWORDS	CHAOS, DAEMON, VERMINLORD, SKAVENTIDE, CLANS VERMINUS, MONSTER, HERO, WIZARD, VERMINLORD WARBRINGER

VERMINLORD WARPSEER

A Verminlord Warpseer is a twisted master of the arcane arts, a rat daemon possessed of sorcerous knowledge fit to drive mortal minds to madness, and the power to unleash screaming maelstroms torn directly from the Realm of Chaos.

MISSILE WEAPONS	Range	Attacks	To Hit	To Wound	Rend	Damage
Prehensile Tails	6"	✹	3+	3+	-1	1
MELEE WEAPONS	Range	Attacks	To Hit	To Wound	Rend	Damage
Doom Glaive	3"	6	3+	✹	-1	D3

DAMAGE TABLE			
Wounds Suffered	Move	Prehensile Tails	Doom Glaive
0-2	12"	4	2+
3-4	10"	3	2+
5-7	8"	2	3+
8-9	6"	1	3+
10+	4"	0	4+

DESCRIPTION

A Verminlord Warpseer is a single model armed with a Doom Glaive and Prehensile Tails.

ABILITIES

The Great Manipulators: *A Warpseer's mind boils with plans and intrigues, labyrinthine schemes overlaying and entangling one another into deranged infinity.*

If this model is on the battlefield at the start of your hero phase, roll a dice. On a 3+, you receive 1 extra command point. On a 6 you receive D3 extra command points instead of 1.

Protection of the Horned Rat: *An eerie sense of watchfulness surrounds this being, and an unholy aura of warding protects them from harm.*

Roll a dice each time you allocate a wound or mortal wound to this model. On a 5+ that wound or mortal wound is negated.

Scry-orb: *Conjured out of nothingness, these swirling orbs can show the Warpseer glimpses of the future, or be hurled into the enemy's midst to explode in shattering clouds of madness.*

You can re-roll save rolls for attacks that target this model. In addition, once per battle, in your shooting phase, you can pick 1 enemy unit within 13" of this model and visible to them. That unit suffers D6 mortal wounds, but you cannot use this ability to re-roll save rolls for this model for the rest of the battle.

Terrifying: *This horrific monstrosity strikes fear deep into the hearts of its enemies.*

Subtract 1 from the Bravery characteristic of enemy units while they are within 3" of any models with this ability.

MAGIC

This model is a **WIZARD**. It can attempt to cast two spells in your hero phase, and attempt to unbind two spells in the enemy hero phase. It knows the Arcane Bolt, Mystic Shield and Dreaded Warpgale spells.

Dreaded Warpgale: *Screeching dark words in an unholy tongue, the Warpseer parts the veil of reality and draws a ravening gale of unnatural energies forth. The skies darken, clouds of glowing madness spill across the heavens, and bolts of warp lightning lash down to blast the rat daemon's enemies into oblivion.*

Dreaded Warpgale has a casting value of 8. If successfully cast, pick 1 enemy unit within 26" of the caster and visible to them. That unit suffers D6 mortal wounds, and run and charge rolls for that unit are halved until your next hero phase. If that unit can fly, it cannot fly until your next hero phase (in addition to having its run and charge rolls halved).

COMMAND ABILITIES

Forth-forth, Children of the Horned Rat!: *Verminlord Warpseers are arch-schemers who take command of skaven swarms to further their labyrinthine plots.*

You can use this command ability at the start of the battleshock phase. If you do so, pick 1 friendly model with this command ability. Do not take battleshock tests for friendly **SKAVEN** units while they are wholly within 26" of that model in that phase.

KEYWORDS	CHAOS, DAEMON, VERMINLORD, SKAVENTIDE, MASTERCLAN, MONSTER, HERO, WIZARD, VERMINLORD WARPSEER

GREY SEER
ON SCREAMING BELL

Mounted atop the creaking carriage of a Screaming Bell, a Grey Seer hurls dark sorcery into the enemy ranks. The ensorcelled bell tolls again and again, its warped peals shattering stone and bone, splintering sanity and rending reality itself.

MELEE WEAPONS	Range	Attacks	To Hit	To Wound	Rend	Damage
Warpstone Staff	2"	3	4+	4+	-1	1
Tearing Claws and Fangs	1"	4	4+	3+	-1	2
Rusty Spikes	1"	D6	✳	3+	-1	1

DAMAGE TABLE			
Wounds Suffered	Move	Rusty Spikes	Peal of Doom
0-3	6"	2+	26"
4-5	6"	3+	22"
6-8	4"	4+	18"
9-10	4"	4+	14"
11+	3"	5+	10"

DESCRIPTION

A Grey Seer on Screaming Bell is a single model armed with a Warpstone Staff.

MOUNT: This model's Screaming Bell attacks with its Rusty Spikes.

CREW: This model has a Rat Ogor crew that attacks with its Tearing Claws and Fangs. For rules purposes, the Rat Ogor is treated in the same manner as a mount.

ABILITIES

Altar of the Horned Rat: *Those skaven that scurry to battle in the shadow of a Screaming Bell are filled with the certainty of victory.*

Do not take battleshock tests for friendly **SKAVENTIDE** units while they are wholly within 13" of this model.

Protection of the Horned Rat: *An eerie sense of watchfulness surrounds this war engine, and an unholy warding protects it from harm.*

Roll a dice each time you allocate a wound or mortal wound to this model. On a 5+ that wound or mortal wound is negated.

Pushed into Battle: *The Screaming Bell's wheeled carriage is heaved into battle by the massed skaven that swarm about it.*

This model cannot move unless it starts the move within 6" of 10 or more friendly **SKAVENTIDE** models. In addition, this model's Rusty Spikes have an Attacks characteristic of 2D6 instead of D6 if this model made a charge move in the same turn.

Peal of Doom: *The ominous tolling of a Screaming Bell resounds above the clamour of battle, crying out 'Doom! Doom! Doom!'.*

At the start of your hero phase, roll 2D6 for this model and look up the result on the table below. The range of the Peal of Doom is shown on the damage table above.

2D6   Result

2   *Magical Backlash:* Each unit within 3" of this model suffers D3 mortal wounds.

3-4   *Unholy Clamour:* Add D6" to this model's Move characteristic until your next hero phase.

5-6   *Deafening Peals:* Roll a dice for each enemy unit within range of this model's Peal of Doom. On a 4+ that unit suffers 1 mortal wound.

7   *Avalanche of Energy:* Until the end of this hero phase, add 1 to casting rolls for friendly **SKAVENTIDE WIZARDS** that are within range of this model's Peal of Doom.

8-9   *Apocalyptic Doom:* Roll a dice for each enemy unit within range of this model's Peal of Doom. On a 4+ that unit suffers D3 mortal wounds.

10-11   *Wall of Unholy Sound:* Until your next hero phase, subtract 1 from hit rolls for attacks made by enemy units while they are wholly within range of this model's Peal of Doom.

12   *A Stirring Beyond the Veil:* You can summon a **VERMINLORD** to the battlefield and add it to your army. The summoned unit must be set up within range of this model's Peal of Doom and more than 9" from any enemy units. If you roll this result a second or subsequent time during a battle, heal up to 12 wounds allocated to this model instead of summoning a **VERMINLORD**.

MAGIC

This model is a **WIZARD**. It can attempt to cast two spells in your hero phase, and attempt to unbind two spells in the enemy hero phase. It knows the Arcane Bolt, Mystic Shield and Cracks Call spells.

Cracks Call: *Harnessing the thunderous peals of the Screaming Bell, the Grey Seer channels a reverberating sorcerous blast into the ground beneath the enemy's feet. Gaping chasms and fume-gouting rents yawn wide, sending screaming victims vanishing into the depths.*

Cracks Call has a casting value of 6. If successfully cast, pick 1 enemy unit within 18" of the caster and visible to them, and roll 2D6. If the roll is greater than that unit's Move characteristic, that unit suffers a number of mortal wounds equal to the difference between its Move characteristic and the roll. This spell has no effect on units that can fly.

KEYWORDS	CHAOS, SKAVEN, SKAVENTIDE, MASTERCLAN, WAR MACHINE, HERO, WIZARD, SCREAMING BELL, GREY SEER

GREY SEER

106

MOVE	6"
WOUNDS	5
SAVE	5+
BRAVERY	6

Grey Seers are manipulators and master sorcerers who attempt to direct the skaven to ultimate victory at any price. They are dangerous and deranged, more than willing to devour raw warpstone in order to supercharge their magical abilities.

MELEE WEAPONS	Range	Attacks	To Hit	To Wound	Rend	Damage
Warpstone Staff	2"	1	4+	3+	-1	D3

DESCRIPTION

A Grey Seer is a single model armed with a Warpstone Staff.

ABILITIES

Warpstone Tokens: *Potentially lethal warpstone is consumed by Grey Seers to aid their spellcasting.*

Once in each of your hero phases, when this model attempts to cast a spell, you can say it will consume a warpstone token before you make the casting roll. If you do so, roll 3D6. This roll cannot be re-rolled or modified. If the 3D6 roll is 13, the spell is cast and cannot be unbound, and after the effects of the spell have been resolved

this model is slain. If the 3D6 roll was not 13, remove 1 dice of your choice, and then use the remaining 2D6 as the casting roll.

MAGIC

This model is a **WIZARD**. It can attempt to cast two spells in your hero phase, and attempt to unbind two spells in the enemy hero phase. It knows the Arcane Bolt, Mystic Shield and Wither spells.

Wither: *The Grey Seer hurls a glowing green globe of magical energy at a foe. Anyone touched by the globe starts to shrivel and wither away.*

Wither has a casting value of 7. If successfully cast, pick 1 enemy unit within 13" of the caster and visible to them, and roll 2D6. If the roll is greater than that unit's Wounds characteristic, that unit suffers D3 mortal wounds. In addition, if the roll is greater than that unit's Wounds characteristic, subtract 1 from hit rolls for attacks made with melee weapons by that unit until your next hero phase.

KEYWORDS	CHAOS, SKAVEN, SKAVENTIDE, MASTERCLAN, HERO, WIZARD, GREY SEER

ARCH-WARLOCK

MOVE	6"
WOUNDS	6
SAVE	3+
BRAVERY	6

The Arch-Warlocks of the Clans Skryre are armour-clad killers whose warp-tech weapons and arcane ability have been the death of countless foes. Though they prefer to lead from the back, Arch-Warlocks are deadly in their own right.

MELEE WEAPONS	Range	Attacks	To Hit	To Wound	Rend	Damage
Stormcage Halberd	2"	1	3+	3+	-2	D3
Piston Claw	1"	1	4+	3+	-2	3

DESCRIPTION

An Arch-Warlock is a single model armed with a Stormcage Halberd and Piston Claw.

ABILITIES

More-more Stormcage!: *A stormcage halberd's generator can be overloaded, if the wielder dares.*

Before you make a hit roll for an attack with a Stormcage Halberd, you can say that the engineer has overloaded its generator. If you do so, the Damage characteristic for that attack is D6 instead of D3. However, if you do so and the unmodified hit roll is 1, that attack fails and this model suffers D6 mortal wounds.

Warpfire Gauntlet: *In an emergency, this weapon can be used to spit a stream of warpfire at the foe.*

Once per battle, in your shooting phase, you can pick 1 enemy unit within 8" of this model and visible to them, and roll a dice. On a 2+ that unit suffers D3 mortal wounds.

MAGIC

This model is a **WIZARD**. It can attempt to cast two spells in your hero phase, and attempt to unbind one spell in the enemy hero phase. It knows the Arcane Bolt, Mystic Shield and Warp Lightning Storm spells.

Warp Lightning Storm: *The Arch-Warlock summons a crackling tempest to kill-smite his foes.*

Warp Lightning Storm has a casting value of 7. If successfully cast, pick up to D3 enemy units within 13" of the caster and visible to them. Those units each suffer D3 mortal wounds. Before making the casting roll, you can say that this model will use its warp-power accumulator to augment the spell. If you do so and the casting attempt is successful and not unbound, the spell inflicts D6 mortal wounds on each of those units instead of D3. However, if you do so and the casting attempt fails or is unbound, this model suffers D3xD6 mortal wounds.

KEYWORDS	CHAOS, SKAVEN, SKAVENTIDE, CLANS SKRYRE, HERO, WIZARD, WARLOCK ENGINEER, ARCH-WARLOCK

WARLOCK ENGINEER

Warlock Engineers scurry into battle with arcane engines strapped to their backs and crackling weapons of war clutched in their gnarled claws. Their warp lightning arcs out to make their victims twitch and dance as it burns them alive.

MISSILE WEAPONS	Range	Attacks	To Hit	To Wound	Rend	Damage
Warplock Pistol	9"	1	3+	3+	-1	D3
MELEE WEAPONS	**Range**	**Attacks**	**To Hit**	**To Wound**	**Rend**	**Damage**
Warp-energy Blade	1"	1	4+	3+	-1	D3

DESCRIPTION

A Warlock Engineer is a single model armed with a Warplock Pistol and Warp-energy Blade.

ABILITIES

More-more Warp-energy!: *A warp-energy blade's generator can be overloaded, if the wielder dares.*

Before you make a hit roll for an attack with a Warp-energy Blade, you can say that the engineer has overloaded its generator. If you do so, the Damage characteristic for that attack is D6 instead of D3. However, if you do so and the unmodified hit roll is 1, that attack fails and this model suffers D6 mortal wounds.

MAGIC

This model is a **WIZARD**. It can attempt to cast one spell in your hero phase, and attempt to unbind one spell in the enemy hero phase. It knows the Warp Lightning spell. Any number of **WARLOCK ENGINEERS** can attempt to cast Warp Lightning spells in the same hero phase.

Warp Lightning: *The engineer points his claw, and bolts of warp lightning arc outwards.*

Warp Lightning has a casting value of 5. If successfully cast, pick 1 enemy unit within 13" of the caster and visible to them. That unit suffers D3 mortal wounds. Before making the casting roll, you can say that this model will use its warp-power accumulator to augment the spell. If you do so and the casting attempt is successful and not unbound, the spell inflicts D6 mortal wounds instead of D3. However, if you do so and the casting attempt fails or is unbound, this model suffers D6 mortal wounds.

KEYWORDS	CHAOS, SKAVEN, SKAVENTIDE, CLANS SKRYRE, HERO, WIZARD, WARLOCK ENGINEER

WARLOCK BOMBARDIER

Warlock Bombardiers are those engineers who develop a particular penchant for weapons that deliver explosive death from extreme range. Their alchemical armaments cause substantial devastation wherever they strike home.

MISSILE WEAPONS	Range	Attacks	To Hit	To Wound	Rend	Damage
Doomrocket	18"	1	4+	3+	-1	D6
MELEE WEAPONS	**Range**	**Attacks**	**To Hit**	**To Wound**	**Rend**	**Damage**
Firing Pole	1"	1	5+	5+	-	1

DESCRIPTION

A Warlock Bombardier is a single model armed with a Doomrocket and Firing Pole.

ABILITIES

More-more Doomrocket!: *A doomrocket's warhead can be overloaded, if the wielder dares.*

Before you make a hit roll for an attack with a Doomrocket, you can say that the engineer has overloaded its warhead. If you do so, the Damage characteristic for that attack is 2D6 instead of D6. However, if you do so and the unmodified hit roll is 1, that attack fails and this model suffers 2D6 mortal wounds.

MAGIC

This model is a **WIZARD**. It can attempt to cast one spell in your hero phase, and attempt to unbind one spell in the enemy hero phase. It knows the Warp Lightning spell. Any number of **WARLOCK ENGINEERS** can attempt to cast Warp Lightning spells in the same hero phase.

Warp Lightning: *The engineer points his claw, and bolts of warp lightning arc outwards.*

Warp Lightning has a casting value of 5. If successfully cast, pick 1 enemy unit within 13" of the caster and visible to them. That unit suffers D3 mortal wounds. Before making the casting roll, you can say that this model will use its warp-power accumulator to augment the spell. If you do so and the casting attempt is successful and not unbound, the spell inflicts D6 mortal wounds instead of D3. However, if you do so and the casting attempt fails or is unbound, this model suffers D6 mortal wounds.

KEYWORDS	CHAOS, SKAVEN, SKAVENTIDE, CLANS SKRYRE, HERO, WIZARD, WARLOCK ENGINEER, WARLOCK BOMBARDIER

MOVE
6"

WOUNDS
6

SAVE
4+

6

BRAVERY

STORMFIENDS

Stormfiends are monstrous fusions of vat-bred Rat Ogors and Skryre contraptions. They are the lumbering shock-troops of the Clans Skryre, and can sweep away entire enemy units in a heartbeat with their vicious wonder-weapons.

MISSILE WEAPONS	Range	Attacks	To Hit	To Wound	Rend	Damage
Ratling Cannons	12"	3D6	4+	3+	-1	1
Windlaunchers	24"	3	4+	4+	-3	D3
Warpfire Projectors	8"			See below		
MELEE WEAPONS	Range	Attacks	To Hit	To Wound	Rend	Damage
Doomflayer Gauntlets	1"	2D3	3+	3+	-2	D3
Grinderfists	1"	4	4+	3+	-2	2
Shock Gauntlets	1"	4	4+	3+	-1	2
Clubbing Blows	1"	4	4+	3+	-	2

DESCRIPTION

A unit of Stormfiends has any number of models. Up to one third of the models in the unit (rounding up) can be armed with one of the following weapon options: Warpfire Projectors and Clubbing Blows; or Windlaunchers and Clubbing Blows.

Up to one third of the models in the unit (rounding up) can be armed with one of the following weapon options: Grinderfists; or Ratling Cannons and Clubbing Blows.

Up to one third of the models in the unit (rounding up) can be armed with one of the following weapon options: Doomflayer Gauntlets and Warpstone-laced Armour; or Shock Gauntlets and Warpstone-laced Armour.

ABILITIES

Doomflayer Gauntlets: *Whirling gyroscopic gears make doomflayer gauntlets especially deadly when the bearer charges at a foe.*

Add 1 to hit rolls for attacks made with Doomflayer Gauntlets if the attacking model made a charge move in the same turn.

Grinderfist Tunnellers: *Grinderfists can be used to create underground tunnels.*

If a unit includes any models equipped with Grinderfists, instead of setting up that unit on the battlefield, you can place it to one side and say that it is set up underground as a reserve unit.

At the end of each of your movement phases, roll a dice for each underground reserve unit. On a 1 or 2, that unit remains underground in reserve (roll for it again in your next movement phase). On a 3+ set up that unit on the battlefield more than 9" from any enemy units.

Any underground reserve units that are still underground and which fail to arrive at the end of your third movement phase suffer D6 mortal wounds. Any surviving models are then set up on the battlefield more than 9" from any enemy units.

Shock Gauntlets: *Sometimes the electrical discharges created by a pair of shock gauntlets create a series of linked explosions.*

If the unmodified hit roll for an attack made with Shock Gauntlets is 6, that attack inflicts D6 hits on that target instead of 1. Make a wound and save roll for each hit.

Warpfire Projectors: *These horrific weapons engulf the target in searing gouts of warpfire.*

Do not use the attack sequence for an attack made with Warpfire Projectors. Instead, roll a dice for each model in the target unit that is within 8" of the attacking model. For each 4+ the target unit suffers 1 mortal wound.

Warpstone-laced Armour: *Stormfiends armed with doomflayer gauntlets or shock gauntlets are protected by heavy plates of warpstone-laced armour.*

A model wearing Warpstone-laced Armour has a Wounds characteristic of 7 instead of 6.

Windlaunchers: *The gas clouds unleashed by a windlauncher engulf even the largest enemy formations in choking poisonous fumes.*

Add 1 to hit rolls for attacks made with Windlaunchers if the target has 10 or more models. In addition, Windlaunchers can target enemy units that are not visible to the attacking model.

KEYWORDS	CHAOS, SKAVEN, SKAVENTIDE, CLANS MOULDER, CLANS SKRYRE, STORMFIENDS

MOVE **3"**
WOUNDS **8**
SAVE **4+**
4
BRAVERY

• WARSCROLL •

WARP LIGHTNING CANNON

109

The Warp Lightning Cannon channels energy from a huge chunk of refined warpstone in order to send roiling blasts of green-and-black lightning hurtling across the battlefield.

MISSILE WEAPONS	Range	Attacks	To Hit	To Wound	Rend	Damage
Warp Lightning Blast	24"	←		See below		→
MELEE WEAPONS	**Range**	**Attacks**	**To Hit**	**To Wound**	**Rend**	**Damage**
Teeth and Knives	1"	D6	5+	5+	-	1

DESCRIPTION

A Warp Lightning Cannon is a single model armed with a Warp Lightning Blast and the crew's Teeth and Knives.

ABILITIES

Warp Lightning Blast: *A Warp Lightning Cannon fires bolts of pure warp lightning that disintegrate any who are caught by them.*

Do not use the attack sequence for an attack made with a Warp Lightning Blast. Instead roll a dice; that roll determines the power of that attack. Then roll 6 more dice. The target suffers 1 mortal wound for each of those rolls that is equal to or greater than the power of that attack.

More-more Warp Lightning!: *A Warlock Engineer can increase the power output of a Warp Lightning Cannon, but at the risk that it will harm the weapon and its crew.*

Before you roll the dice that determines the power of a Warp Lightning Blast for this model, if there is a friendly **WARLOCK ENGINEER** within 3" of this model you can say that the engineer will increase the weapon's power output. If you do so, roll 12 more dice instead of 6 more dice for that attack. However, after the attack has been resolved, this model suffers D3 mortal wounds for each unmodified roll of 1 on those 12 dice. A single **WARLOCK ENGINEER** cannot be used to increase the power output of more than one Warp Lightning Blast in the same phase.

KEYWORDS	CHAOS, SKAVEN, SKAVENTIDE, CLANS SKRYRE, WAR MACHINE, WARP LIGHTNING CANNON

MOVE **6"**
WOUNDS **1**
SAVE **6+**
4
BRAVERY

• WARSCROLL •

SKRYRE ACOLYTES

The Acolytes of the Clans Skryre go to war amidst the tinny wheeze of metal bellows and the perilous clink of poisoned wind globes rattling together. They hurl volleys of these lethal spheres, which shatter in the foe's midst and choke them horribly to death.

MISSILE WEAPONS	Range	Attacks	To Hit	To Wound	Rend	Damage
Poisoned Wind Globe	8"	1	4+	4+	-2	D3
MELEE WEAPONS	**Range**	**Attacks**	**To Hit**	**To Wound**	**Rend**	**Damage**
Rusty Knife	1"	1	5+	5+	-	1

DESCRIPTION

A unit of Skryre Acolytes can have any number of models, each armed with a Poisoned Wind Globe and Rusty Knife.

ABILITIES

Quick-quick Volley!: *Skryre Acolytes look for opportunities to run forwards and lob their deadly missiles.*

This unit can run and still shoot later in the same turn.

Gas Clouds: *Poisoned wind globes are glass or crystal orbs filled with deadly warpstone gas that can engulf an enemy regiment.*

Add 1 to hit rolls for attacks made with a Poisoned Wind Globe if the target unit has 10 or more models.

KEYWORDS	CHAOS, SKAVEN, SKAVENTIDE, CLANS SKRYRE, SKRYRE ACOLYTES

DOOMWHEEL

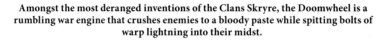

110

MOVE **4D6"**

WOUNDS **8**

SAVE **4+**

BRAVERY **7**

Amongst the most deranged inventions of the Clans Skryre, the Doomwheel is a rumbling war engine that crushes enemies to a bloody paste while spitting bolts of warp lightning into their midst.

MISSILE WEAPONS	Range	Attacks	To Hit	To Wound	Rend	Damage
Warp Bolts	13"	D6	3+	3+	-1	D3
MELEE WEAPONS	**Range**	**Attacks**	**To Hit**	**To Wound**	**Rend**	**Damage**
Grinding Wheel	1"	D6	3+	3+	-1	1
Teeth and Knives	1"	6	5+	5+	-	1

DESCRIPTION

A Doomwheel is a single model armed with Warp Bolts, a Grinding Wheel and its crew's Teeth and Knives.

ABILITIES

Rolling Doom: *A Doomwheel will mercilessly crush anything in its path.*

When this model makes a normal move, it can pass across models with a Wounds characteristic of 3 or less in the same manner as a model that can fly. In addition, after this model has made a normal move or a charge move, roll a dice for each unit that has any models it passed across, and each other unit that is within 1" of this model at the end of the move. On a 2+ that unit suffers D3 mortal wounds.

More-more Speed!: *The Warlock Engineer that pilots a Doomwheel can goad the rats that propel it in order to make it move faster, but at the risk that they will turn and attack their tormentor.*

When this model makes a normal move, you can re-roll the 4D6 roll that determines its Move characteristic. However, if you do so and the new roll includes any dice with an unmodified roll of 1, then your opponent carries out that normal move for that model instead of you.

More-more Warp Bolts!: *A daring or foolhardy engineer pilot can overload their Doomwheel's warp lightning generator.*

Before you determine the Attacks characteristic for this model's Warp Bolts attack, you can say that the engineer is overcharging the warp lightning generator. If you do so, the Attacks characteristic for that attack is 2D6 instead of D6. However, if you do so and you roll a double, this model suffers 2D6 mortal wounds after all of the attacks have been resolved.

KEYWORDS	CHAOS, SKAVEN, SKAVENTIDE, CLANS SKRYRE, WAR MACHINE, DOOMWHEEL

WARPLOCK JEZZAILS

Long-barrelled rifles that fire glowing warp-bullets from behind bulky pavises, Warplock Jezzails are so sizeable that they require two trained skaven to operate, and can blast an armoured cavalryman from their saddle at thirteen hundred paces.

MISSILE WEAPONS	Range	Attacks	To Hit	To Wound	Rend	Damage
Warplock Jezzail	30"	1	4+	3+	-2	2
MELEE WEAPONS	Range	Attacks	To Hit	To Wound	Rend	Damage
Rusty Knives	1"	2	5+	5+	-	1

DESCRIPTION

A unit of Warplock Jezzails has any number of models, each armed with a Warplock Jezzail and Rusty Knives.

ABILITIES

Warpstone Snipers: *The Warplock Jezzail fires a bullet made of highly toxic warpstone.*

If the unmodified hit roll for an attack made with a Warplock Jezzail is 6, that attack inflicts 2 mortal wounds on the target and the attack sequence ends (do not make a wound or save roll).

Pavise: *The pavise carried by a Warplock Jezzail team shields them from harm, and can be used to steady their long-barrelled weapon.*

You can re-roll hit rolls for attacks made with this unit's Warplock Jezzails if this unit has not made a move in the same turn. In addition, add 2 to save rolls for attacks made with missile weapons that target this unit.

KEYWORDS CHAOS, SKAVEN, SKAVENTIDE, CLANS SKRYRE, WARPLOCK JEZZAILS

RATLING GUN

When its handle is cranked, the Ratling Gun's barrels whir up to speed with a scream. The weapon spits warp-laced bullets into the enemy, mowing down foe after foe – at least until it detonates with a sound like a bomb going off in a clockmaker's workshop.

MISSILE WEAPONS	Range	Attacks	To Hit	To Wound	Rend	Damage
Ratling Gun	12"	2D6	4+	4+	-1	1
MELEE WEAPONS	Range	Attacks	To Hit	To Wound	Rend	Damage
Rusty Knives	1"	2	5+	5+	-	1

DESCRIPTION

A Ratling Gun is a single model armed with a Ratling Gun and Rusty Knives.

ABILITIES

More-more Warplead!: *A Ratling Gun's crew can release its gimbal-limiter, increasing the gun's rate of fire at the risk of a catastrophic malfunction.*

Before you determine the Attacks characteristic for this model's Ratling Gun, you can say that the crew are releasing its gimbal-limiter. If you do so, double the Attacks characteristic for that attack. However, if you do so and the roll that determines the Attacks characteristic is a double, this model is slain after all of the attacks have been resolved.

KEYWORDS CHAOS, SKAVEN, SKAVENTIDE, CLANS SKRYRE, WEAPON TEAM, RATLING GUN

WARPFIRE THROWER

MOVE 6"
WOUNDS 3
SAVE 6+
BRAVERY 4

112

The Warpfire Thrower is a truly horrific and highly unstable weapon that fires jetting sheets of sticky warpstone-infused oils. These ignite upon contact with air and burn furiously through flesh, stone, metal and bone.

MISSILE WEAPONS	Range	Attacks	To Hit	To Wound	Rend	Damage
Warpfire Thrower	8"			See below		
MELEE WEAPONS	**Range**	**Attacks**	**To Hit**	**To Wound**	**Rend**	**Damage**
Rusty Knives	1"	2	5+	5+	-	1

DESCRIPTION

A Warpfire Thrower is a single model armed with a Warpfire Thrower and Rusty Knives.

ABILITIES

Warpfire: *These horrific weapons engulf the target in searing gouts of warpfire.*

Do not use the attack sequence for an attack made with a Warpfire Thrower. Instead, roll a dice for each model in the target unit that is within 8" of the attacking model. For each 4+ the target unit suffers 1 mortal wound.

More-more Warpfire!: *A Warpfire Thrower's crew can disable the weapon's flow regulator, allowing it to unleash great, uncontrolled gouts of warpfire but at the risk of immolating themselves.*

Before you pick the target for this model's Warpfire Thrower, you can say that the crew are disabling the flow regulator. If you do so, roll 2 dice for each enemy model within 8" of this model instead of 1 dice. However, if you do so, you must roll a dice after the dice have been rolled to see if the Warpfire Thrower inflicts any mortal wounds, and on a 1 or 2 this model is slain.

KEYWORDS | CHAOS, SKAVEN, SKAVENTIDE, CLANS SKRYRE, WEAPON TEAM, WARPFIRE THROWER

Skryre weapon teams scuttle to the front lines to unleash destruction upon the enemy. Doom-Flayer and Warp-Grinder mechanisms whir in preparation for the kill, while the Warpfire Thrower's unstable fuel roars to a boil.

DOOM-FLAYER

MOVE 2D6"
WOUNDS 3
SAVE 5+
BRAVERY 4

113

The Doom-Flayer rumbles across the battlefield in a whirling blur of blades, its crew seeking to close the distance to the foe with un-skavenlike eagerness. When its charge hits home, the bloody carnage that ensues is hideous to behold.

MELEE WEAPONS	Range	Attacks	To Hit	To Wound	Rend	Damage
Whirling Blades	1"	D6	3+	3+	-1	1
Rusty Knives	1"	2	5+	5+	-	1

DESCRIPTION

A Doom-Flayer is a single model armed with Whirling Blades and Rusty Knives.

ABILITIES

Whirling Death: *Doom-Flayers crash into the foe with hellish results, leaving a trail of gore in their wake.*

Add 1 to hit rolls for attacks made with this model's Whirling Blades if this model made a charge move in the same turn.

More-more Whirling Death: *A daring or deranged crew can kick the warpstone generator that powers their Doom-Flayer into overdrive. Sometimes they even survive the experience.*

Before you determine the Attacks characteristic for this model's Whirling Blades, you can say that the crew have kicked its generator into overdrive. If you do so, roll 2D6 to determine the Attacks characteristic for that attack instead of D6. However, if you do so and the roll that determines the Attacks characteristic is either a double or a roll of 7, this model is slain after all of the attacks have been resolved.

KEYWORDS | CHAOS, SKAVEN, SKAVENTIDE, CLANS SKRYRE, WEAPON TEAM, DOOM-FLAYER

WARP-GRINDER

MOVE 6"
WOUNDS 3
SAVE 6+
BRAVERY 4

The Warp-Grinder uses an energised warp-prong to burn smoking black tunnels through solid rock, and any enemy stupid enough to stand in its way. They are both weapons and a means to infiltrate the battlefield.

MELEE WEAPONS	Range	Attacks	To Hit	To Wound	Rend	Damage
Warp-Grinder	1"	1	4+	3+	-2	2

DESCRIPTION

A Warp-Grinder is a single model armed with a Warp-Grinder.

ABILITIES

Tunnel Skulkers: *A Warp-Grinder can be used to bore a subterranean tunnel, allowing a clawpack following it to get behind enemy lines.*

Instead of setting up this model on the battlefield, you can place this model to one side and say that it is set up tunnelling as a reserve unit. If you do so, when you would set up another friendly **SKAVENTIDE** unit that is not a **MONSTER** or a **WAR MACHINE**, instead of setting up that unit on the battlefield, you can say that it is joining this model tunnelling as a reserve unit. Only 1 unit can join this model in this way.

At the end of any of your movement phases, if this model is tunnelling, it can arrive on the battlefield. If it does so, set up this model anywhere on the battlefield more than 9" from any enemy models, and then set up any unit that joined this model wholly within 13" of this model and more than 9" from any enemy models. Then roll a dice for this model and any unit that joined it. On a 1 or 2, that unit suffers D6 mortal wounds.

Any tunnelling reserve units that fail to arrive on the battlefield before the start of your fourth movement phase are destroyed.

KEYWORDS | CHAOS, SKAVEN, SKAVENTIDE, CLANS SKRYRE, WEAPON TEAM, WARP-GRINDER

MOVE	6"
WOUNDS	5
SAVE	5+
BRAVERY	6

PLAGUE PRIEST

Plague Priests shriek blasphemous prayers that unleash the dark diseases of the Great Corruptor upon their foes. Those not wasted away or withered into ooze are swiftly slain by blows from the priests' warpstone-capped staves and smog-belching censers.

MELEE WEAPONS	Range	Attacks	To Hit	To Wound	Rend	Damage
Warpstone-tipped Staff	2"	1	4+	3+	-1	D3
Plague Censer	2"	2	4+	3+	-1	1

DESCRIPTION

A Plague Priest is a single model armed with a Warpstone-tipped Staff and a Plague Censer.

ABILITIES

Plague Prayers: *Plague Priests can beseech the Horned Rat to unleash dread maladies on the foe.*

In your hero phase, this model can chant one of the following prayers. If it does so, pick 1 of the prayers and then make a prayer roll by rolling a dice. On a 1, this model suffers 1 mortal wound and the prayer is not answered. On a 2, the prayer is not answered. On a 3+ the prayer is answered.

Disease-disease!: If this prayer is answered, pick 1 enemy unit within 13" of this model, and roll 1 dice for each model in that unit. For each 6, that unit suffers 1 mortal wound. This prayer has no effect on **Clans Pestilens** units.

Pestilence-pestilence!: If this prayer is answered, pick a point on the battlefield that is within 13" of this model. Roll a dice for each unit within 3" of that point. On 4+ that unit suffers D3 mortal wounds. This prayer has no effect on **Clans Pestilens** units.

Frenzied Assault: *The presence of the enemy drives this crazed warrior into a terrible rage.*

Add 1 to the Attacks characteristic of this model's melee weapons if this model made a charge move in the same turn.

Poisonous Fumes: *Plague censers emit huge clouds of noxious gas.*

At the end of the combat phase, roll 1 dice for each unit within 3" of any units with this ability. On a 4+ the unit being rolled for suffers 1 mortal wound. On a 6 that unit suffers D3 mortal wounds instead of 1. This ability has no effect on **Clans Pestilens** units.

KEYWORDS	CHAOS, SKAVEN, SKAVENTIDE, NURGLE, CLANS PESTILENS, HERO, PRIEST, PLAGUE PRIEST

MOVE	3"
WOUNDS	6
SAVE	5+
BRAVERY	4

PLAGUECLAW

Rotten wood creaks as the throwing arm of the Plagueclaw is cranked slowly back. Foul plague-slop is loaded into the weapon's claw, before being launched in a high arc to rain infectious filth down upon the enemy lines.

MISSILE WEAPONS	Range	Attacks	To Hit	To Wound	Rend	Damage
Plagueclaw Catapult	6-31"	1	3+	3+	-2	D6
MELEE WEAPONS	Range	Attacks	To Hit	To Wound	Rend	Damage
Rusty Knives	1"	D6	5+	5+	-	1

DESCRIPTION

A Plagueclaw is a single model armed with a Plagueclaw Catapult and Rusty Knives.

ABILITIES

Barrage of Disease: *A Plagueclaw hurls great globs of diseased filth at its targets.*

A Plagueclaw Catapult can target enemy units that are not visible to the attacking model. In addition, add 1 to hit rolls and increase the Damage characteristic to 2D6 for attacks made with a Plagueclaw Catapult if the target has 10 or more models.

Hideous Death: *Those splashed by this weapon's semi-congealed liquid ammunition die horribly, their skin sloughing off in clumps and their bodies erupting in glistening sores.*

Subtract 1 from the Bravery characteristic of a unit targeted by any Plagueclaw Catapults until the end of the turn.

KEYWORDS	CHAOS, SKAVEN, SKAVENTIDE, NURGLE, CLANS PESTILENS, WAR MACHINE, PLAGUECLAW

PLAGUE PRIEST
ON PLAGUE FURNACE

The huge censer of the Plague Furnace roars low and loud as it swings ominously back and forth. Clouds of billowing smog roll from within to shroud the foe in choking foulness even as the Plague Priest riding the carriage shrieks his twisted prayers.

MELEE WEAPONS	Range	Attacks	To Hit	To Wound	Rend	Damage
Great Plague Censer	3"			See below		
Warpstone-tipped Staff	2"	1	4+	3+	-1	D3
Foetid Blades	1"	6	4+	4+	-	1
Rusty Spikes	1"	D6	✷	3+	-1	1

DAMAGE TABLE			
Wounds Suffered	Move	Great Plague Censer	Rusty Spikes
0-3	6"	D3+4	2+
4-5	6"	D3+3	3+
6-8	4"	D3+2	4+
9-10	4"	D3+1	4+
11+	3"	D3	5+

DESCRIPTION

A Plague Priest on Plague Furnace is a single model armed with a Warpstone-tipped Staff.

MOUNT: This model's Plague Furnace attacks with its Great Plague Censer and Rusty Spikes.

CREW: This model has a Plague Monk crew that attacks with their Foetid Blades. For rules purposes, the crew are treated in the same manner as a mount.

ABILITIES

Altar of the Horned Rat: *Those skaven that scurry to battle in the twisted shadow of a Plague Furnace are wreathed in potent fumes that fill them with unnatural courage.*

Do not take battleshock tests for friendly **SKAVENTIDE** units while they are wholly within 13" of this model.

Great Plague Censer: *Once a Plague Furnace is engaged in combat, its mighty swinging plague censer is let loose, sending the giant spiked ball of death crashing into enemy formations.*

Do not use the attack sequence for an attack made with this model's Great Plague Censer. Instead pick 1 enemy unit within 3" of this model and roll a dice. On a 2+ that unit suffers a number of mortal wounds equal to the Great Plague Censer value shown on the damage table above.

Noxious Prayers: *The Plague Priest that rides atop a Plague Furnace can pray for diseases to bless his followers.*

In your hero phase, this model can chant one of the following prayers. If it does so, pick 1 of the prayers and then make a prayer roll by rolling a dice. On a 1, this model suffers 1 mortal wound and the prayer is not answered. On a 2, the prayer is not answered. On a 3+ the prayer is answered.

Filth-filth!: If this prayer is answered, pick 1 friendly **CLANS PESTILENS** unit wholly within 13" of this model. You can re-roll wound rolls for attacks made by that unit until your next hero phase.

Rabid-rabid!: If this prayer is answered, pick 1 friendly **CLANS PESTILENS** unit wholly within 13" of this model. Add 1 to the Attacks characteristic of melee weapons used by that unit until your next hero phase. You cannot pick the same unit to be affected by this prayer more than once per hero phase.

Poisonous Fumes: *Plague censers emit huge clouds of noxious gas.*

At the end of the combat phase, roll 1 dice for each unit within 3" of any units with this ability. On a 4+ the unit being rolled for suffers 1 mortal wound. On a 6 that unit suffers D3 mortal wounds instead of 1. This ability has no effect on **CLANS PESTILENS** units.

Protection of the Horned Rat: *An eerie sense of watchfulness surrounds this war engine, and an unholy warding protects it from harm.*

Roll a dice each time you allocate a wound or mortal wound to this model. On a 5+ that wound or mortal wound is negated.

Pushed into Battle: *The wheeled carriage that supports a Plague Furnace must be pushed into battle by a teeming horde of skaven.*

This model cannot move unless it starts the move within 6" of 10 or more friendly **SKAVENTIDE** models. In addition, this model's Rusty Spikes have an Attacks characteristic of 2D6 instead of D6 if this model made a charge move in the same turn.

KEYWORDS	CHAOS, SKAVEN, SKAVENTIDE, NURGLE, CLANS PESTILENS, WAR MACHINE, HERO, PRIEST, PLAGUE FURNACE, PLAGUE PRIEST

116

MOVE 6"
WOUNDS 1
SAVE 6+
BRAVERY 5

PLAGUE MONKS

Driven into battle by their frenzied faith, Plague Monks overwhelm their enemies in a pestilential mass. They hack and stab wildly with their foetid blades, spreading disease and infection with every blow.

MELEE WEAPONS	Range	Attacks	To Hit	To Wound	Rend	Damage
Foetid Blade	1"	2	4+	4+	-	1
Woe-stave	2"	1	4+	5+	-	1

DESCRIPTION

A unit of Plague Monks has any number of models. The unit is armed with one of the following weapon options: a pair of Foetid Blades; or a Foetid Blade and Woe-stave.

BRINGER-OF-THE-WORD: 1 model in this unit can be a Bringer-of-the-Word. That model replaces its weapon option with a Foetid Blade and carries a Book of Woes.

STANDARD BEARERS: 1 in every 20 models in this unit can either be a Contagion Banner Bearer or an Icon of Pestilence Bearer.

Contagion Banner: Roll a dice each time a model from this unit is slain by an attack made with a melee weapon if this unit includes any Contagion Banner Bearers, before the slain model is removed. On a 6 the attacking unit suffers 1 mortal wound after all of its attacks have been resolved.

Icon of Pestilence: If the unmodified wound roll for an attack made with a melee weapon by a model from this unit is 6 while this unit includes any Icon of Pestilence Bearers, add 1 to the damage inflicted by that attack.

PLAGUE HARBINGERS: 1 in every 20 models in this unit can either be a Doom Gong Bearer or a Bale-chime Bearer.

Doom Gong: Add 1 to run and charge rolls for this unit while it includes any Doom Gong Bearers.

Bale-chime: If the unmodified hit roll for an attack made with a melee weapon by a model from this unit is 6 while this unit includes any Bale-chime Bearers, improve the Rend characteristic for that attack by 1.

ABILITIES

Pair of Foetid Blades: *Plague Monks armed with a pair of foetid blades slash furiously at the foe with little concern for their own protection.*

You can re-roll hit rolls for attacks made with a pair of Foetid Blades.

Frenzied Assault: *The presence of the enemy drives these crazed warriors into a terrible rage.*

Add 1 to the Attacks characteristic of this unit's melee weapons if this unit made a charge move in the same turn.

Book of Woes: *The champions of the Plague Monks lead their followers in recitations from foul Books of Woes, endlessly repeating the Liturgus Infectus and Rite of Infection, calling upon the Horned Rat to strike down the enemy with disease.*

In your hero phase, you can pick 1 enemy unit within 13" of this unit's Bringer-of-the-Word and roll a dice. On a 4+ that unit suffers 1 mortal wound. On a 6 that unit suffers D3 mortal wounds instead of 1. This ability has no effect on CLANS PESTILENS units.

KEYWORDS	CHAOS, SKAVEN, SKAVENTIDE, NURGLE, CLANS PESTILENS, PLAGUE MONKS

PLAGUE CENSER BEARERS

Plague Censer Bearers rush forwards in a foaming frenzy. Maddened by disease, they swing their weapons in devastating arcs, crunching armour, flesh and bone. Few can long endure their assault, or the choking clouds of plague-smog that accompany it.

MELEE WEAPONS	Range	Attacks	To Hit	To Wound	Rend	Damage
Plague Censer	2"	2	4+	3+	-1	1

DESCRIPTION
A unit of Plague Censer Bearers has any number of models, each armed with a Plague Censer.

ABILITIES
Frenzied Assault: *The presence of the enemy drives these crazed warriors into a terrible rage.*

Add 1 to the Attacks characteristic of this unit's melee weapons if this unit made a charge move in the same turn.

Plague Disciples: *Plague Censer Bearers become even more frenzied in the presence of their zealous brethren.*

You can re-roll hit rolls for attacks made by this unit while it is wholly within 18" of any friendly **PLAGUE MONKS** units. In addition, you can re-roll battleshock tests for this unit while it is wholly within 18" of any friendly **PLAGUE MONKS** units.

Poisonous Fumes: *Plague censers emit huge clouds of noxious gas.*

At the end of the combat phase, roll 1 dice for each unit within 3" of any units with this ability. On a 4+ the unit being rolled for suffers 1 mortal wound. On a 6 that unit suffers D3 mortal wounds instead of 1. This ability has no effect on **CLANS PESTILENS** units.

KEYWORDS	CHAOS, SKAVEN, SKAVENTIDE, NURGLE, CLANS PESTILENS, PLAGUE CENSER BEARERS

CLAWLORD

Verminus Clawlords are powerful fighters and cunning leaders, exhorting their chittering followers to overrun the enemy lines. They are most dangerous when caught at bay, for they will fight for their lives with frantic ferocity.

MELEE WEAPONS	Range	Attacks	To Hit	To Wound	Rend	Damage
Warpforged Blade	1"	3	3+	3+	-1	D3

DESCRIPTION
A Clawlord is a single model armed with a Warpforged Blade.

ABILITIES
Cornered Fury: *A Clawlord that is in fear for his life fights with unbridled ferocity.*

Add the number of wounds allocated to this model to the Attacks characteristic of this model's melee weapons.

COMMAND ABILITIES
Gnash-gnaw on their Bones!: *At a Clawlord's command, his minions hurl themselves at the foe.*

You can use this command ability at the start of the combat phase. If you do so, pick 1 friendly **CLANS VERMINUS** unit wholly within 13" of a friendly model with this command ability. Add 1 to the Attacks characteristic of melee weapons used by that unit in that phase. You cannot pick the same unit to benefit from this ability more than once per phase.

KEYWORDS	CHAOS, SKAVEN, SKAVENTIDE, CLANS VERMINUS, HERO, CLAWLORD

SKRITCH SPITECLAW

MOVE 6"
WOUNDS 5
SAVE 4+
BRAVERY 6

Skritch Spiteclaw is a particularly cunning skaven warlord who has assembled an impressive horde of cut-throat vermin to serve his will. Though he prefers that his minions fight and die on his behalf, when cornered, Skritch becomes a whirling dervish of spiked steel and ripping claws.

MELEE WEAPONS	Range	Attacks	To Hit	To Wound	Rend	Damage
Wicked Halberd	2"	3	3+	3+	-1	D3

DESCRIPTION

Skritch Spiteclaw is a named character that is a single model. He is armed with a Wicked Halberd.

ABILITIES

There are Always More: *Skaven warlords gladly hurl their warriors into the blades of the enemy, content in the knowledge that there are always more Clanrat lives to sacrifice.*

At the start of your hero phase, if this model is within 13" of a friendly **Spiteclaw's Swarm**, you can return D3 slain models to that unit (you cannot return Krrk the Almost-trusted). Set up the returning models one at a time within 1" of a model from that unit (this can be a model you returned to the unit earlier in the same phase). Returning models can only be set up within 3" of an enemy unit if one or more models from the same unit are already within 3" of that enemy unit.

COMMAND ABILITIES

Gnash-gnaw on their Bones!: *At a Clawlord's command, his minions hurl themselves at the foe.*

You can use this command ability at the start of the combat phase. If you do so, pick 1 friendly **Clans Verminus** unit wholly within 13" of a friendly model with this command ability. Add 1 to the Attacks characteristic of melee weapons used by that unit in that phase. You cannot pick the same unit to benefit from this ability more than once per phase.

KEYWORDS | CHAOS, SKAVEN, SKAVENTIDE, CLANS VERMINUS, HERO, CLAWLORD, SKRITCH SPITECLAW

SPITECLAW'S SWARM

MOVE 6"
WOUNDS 1
SAVE 6+
BRAVERY 4

Skritch Spiteclaw entrusts the command and discipline of his verminous ranks to the sadistic taskmaster Krrk the Almost-trusted. Though for now he is content to spend skaven lives at his master's command, the foul-spirited Krrk has his own ambitious schemes for power.

MELEE WEAPONS	Range	Attacks	To Hit	To Wound	Rend	Damage
Festering Skaven's Stabbing Blades	1"	2	4+	4+	-	1
Hungering Skaven's Rusty Flail	1"	1	4+	4+	-	1
Krrk's Rusty Spear	2"	2	4+	4+	-	1
Lurking Skaven's Punch Daggers	1"	2	4+	4+	-	1

DESCRIPTION

Spiteclaw's Swarm consists of 4 models. One model is Krrk the Almost-trusted, armed with a Rusty Spear; one model is armed with a Rusty Flail; one model is armed with Stabbing Blades; and one model is armed with Punch Daggers.

KRRK THE ALMOST-TRUSTED: The leader of this unit is Krrk the Almost-trusted. Do not take battleshock tests for this unit while it includes Krrk the Almost-trusted. In addition, if Skritch Spiteclaw is slain, add 2 to the Attacks characteristic of Krrk's Rusty Spear for the rest of this battle.

ABILITIES

Aversion to Death: *Blessed with swift reactions, Spiteclaw's Swarm are quick to scamper out of the path of enemy attacks.*

After the first wound or mortal wound is allocated to this unit in any phase, you can roll a dice each time you allocate a further wound or mortal wound to this unit in that phase. On a 5+ that wound or mortal wound is negated.

KEYWORDS | CHAOS, SKAVEN, SKAVENTIDE, CLANS VERMINUS, SPITECLAW'S SWARM

CLANRATS

MOVE	6"	
WOUNDS	1	SAVE 6+
BRAVERY	4	

Clanrats mass into huge clawpacks, their vast numbers bolstering their courage and allowing them to surge across the battlefield and overwhelm the enemy regardless of the hideous casualties they suffer along the way.

MELEE WEAPONS	Range	Attacks	To Hit	To Wound	Rend	Damage
Rusty Spear	2"	1	5+	4+	-	1
Rusty Blade	1"	1	4+	4+	-	1

DESCRIPTION

A unit of Clanrats has any number of models. The unit is armed with one of the following weapon options: Rusty Spear; or Rusty Blade. Some units of Clanrats also carry Clanshields.

CLAWLEADER: 1 model in this unit can be a Clawleader. Add 1 to the Attacks characteristic of that model's melee weapons.

CLANRAT STANDARD BEARER: 1 in every 20 models in this unit can be a Clanrat Standard Bearer. This unit can retreat and still charge later in the same turn while it includes any Clanrat Standard Bearers.

CLANRAT BELL-RINGER: 1 in every 20 models in this unit can be a Clanrat Bell-ringer. Add 2 to run rolls for this unit while it includes any Clanrat Bell-ringers.

ABILITIES

Clanshields: *The shields carried by skaven warriors are rickety and slipshod, but can still be used to form a barrier to turn aside blows.*

Add 1 to save rolls for attacks that target a unit that carries Clanshields while it has 10 or more models.

KEYWORDS | CHAOS, SKAVEN, SKAVENTIDE, CLANS VERMINUS, CLANRATS

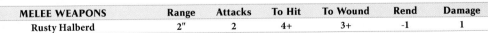

STORMVERMIN

MOVE	6"	
WOUNDS	1	SAVE 5+
BRAVERY	5	

Burly skaven warriors clad in clanking armour and wielding wickedly sharp halberds, Stormvermin are the swaggering elite of the Clans Verminus. In sufficient numbers, they can hack their way through an enemy battle line amidst welters of gore.

MELEE WEAPONS	Range	Attacks	To Hit	To Wound	Rend	Damage
Rusty Halberd	2"	2	4+	3+	-1	1

DESCRIPTION

A unit of Stormvermin has any number of models, each armed with a Rusty Halberd. Some units of Stormvermin also carry Clanshields.

FANGLEADER: 1 model in this unit can be a Fangleader. Add 1 to the Attacks characteristic of that model's Rusty Halberd.

STORMVERMIN STANDARD BEARER: 1 in every 10 models in this unit can be a Stormvermin Standard Bearer. This unit can retreat and still charge later in the same turn while it includes any Stormvermin Standard Bearers.

STORMVERMIN DRUMMER: 1 in every 10 models in this unit can be a Stormvermin Drummer. Add 2 to run rolls for this unit while it includes any Stormvermin Drummers.

ABILITIES

Clanshields: *The shields carried by skaven warriors are rickety and slipshod, but can still be used to form a barrier to turn aside blows.*

Add 1 to save rolls for attacks that target a unit that carries Clanshields while it has 10 or more models.

KEYWORDS | CHAOS, SKAVEN, SKAVENTIDE, CLANS VERMINUS, STORMVERMIN

PACKMASTERS

MOVE 6"
WOUNDS 2
SAVE 6+
BRAVERY 5

120

The Packmasters of the Clans Moulder ply their lashes and their snapping things-catchers to goad their war beasts into battle. Should the foe stray close, those same vicious weapons are readily turned upon them, too.

MELEE WEAPONS	Range	Attacks	To Hit	To Wound	Rend	Damage
Herding Whip	3"	1	4+	4+	-	1
Rusty Blade	1"	2	4+	4+	-	1
Things-catcher	2"	1	4+	4+	-1	2

DESCRIPTION

A unit of Packmasters has any number of models, each armed with a Herding Whip and Rusty Blade. 1 in every 3 models can replace their Rusty Blade with a Things-catcher.

ABILITIES

Crack the Whip: *Packmasters use their whips to drive their fighting beasts into a battle frenzy.*

Add 1 to hit rolls for attacks made with melee weapons by friendly **CLANS MOULDER PACK** units while they are wholly within 12" of any models with this ability. In addition, double the Bravery characteristic of friendly **CLANS MOULDER PACK** units while they are wholly within 12" of any models with this ability.

KEYWORDS	CHAOS, SKAVEN, SKAVENTIDE, CLANS MOULDER, PACKMASTERS

MASTER MOULDER

MOVE 6"
WOUNDS 5
SAVE 5+
BRAVERY 6

Master Moulders are twisted and cruel. Theirs are the deranged minds behind the creation of the Clans Moulders' horrific war beasts, and at their command pack after pack of those foul fiends can be unleashed upon the foe.

MELEE WEAPONS	Range	Attacks	To Hit	To Wound	Rend	Damage
Warpstone-tipped Lash	3"	6	3+	4+	-1	1
Things-catcher	2"	4	4+	4+	-1	2

DESCRIPTION

A Master Moulder is a single model armed with a Warpstone-tipped Lash or a Things-catcher.

ABILITIES

Master Moulder: *These burly commanders are the breeders, mutators and healers of Clans Moulder.*

In your hero phase, you can pick 1 friendly **CLANS MOULDER PACK** model within 3" of this model. Heal D3 wounds allocated to that model.

Crack the Whip: *Master Moulders use their whips to drive their fighting beasts into a battle frenzy.*

Add 1 to hit rolls for attacks made with melee weapons by friendly **CLANS MOULDER PACK** units while they are wholly within 12" of any models with this ability. In addition, double the Bravery characteristic of friendly **CLANS MOULDER PACK** units while they are wholly within 12" of any models with this ability.

COMMAND ABILITIES

Unleash More-more Beasts!: *A Master Moulder can order forth more packs of fighting beasts if the tide of battle starts to turn against them.*

You can use this command ability when a friendly **CLANS MOULDER PACK** unit is destroyed if a friendly model with this command ability is on the battlefield. If you do so, roll a dice. On a 5+ a new unit identical to the one that was destroyed is added to your army. Set up the new unit wholly within your territory and wholly within 6" of the edge of the battlefield, more than 9" from any enemy units. You cannot use this command ability more than once per phase.

KEYWORDS	CHAOS, SKAVEN, SKAVENTIDE, CLANS MOULDER, HERO, MASTER MOULDER

MOVE 2D6"
WOUNDS 12
SAVE 5+
BRAVERY 6

HELL PIT ABOMINATION

Living nightmares, Hell Pit Abominations are misshapen monstrosities of immense size that squirm, lurch and drag their way into battle. Their grotesque assemblages of snapping jaws, lashing talons and crushing fists make short work of the foe.

MELEE WEAPONS	Range	Attacks	To Hit	To Wound	Rend	Damage
Gnashing Teeth	1"	6	3+	3+	✴	2
Flailing Fists	2"	✴	3+	3+	-1	3
Avalanche of Flesh	1"	←		See below		→

DAMAGE TABLE			
Wounds Suffered	Gnashing Teeth	Flailing Fists	Avalanche of Flesh
0-2	-3	6	2+
3-4	-2	5	3+
5-6	-2	4	4+
7-8	-1	3	5+
10+	-1	2	6+

DESCRIPTION

A Hell Pit Abomination is a single model armed with Gnashing Teeth, Flailing Fists and an Avalanche of Flesh.

ABILITIES

Avalanche of Flesh: *A Hell Pit Abomination can rear up to its fullest height before crashing back to the ground, crushing foes beneath its sickening bulk.*

Do not use the attack sequence for an attack made with an Avalanche of Flesh. Instead, roll a number of dice equal to the number of models from the target unit within 3" of the attacking model. You can re-roll any of the dice if this model made a charge move in the same turn. The target unit suffers 1 mortal wound for each roll that is equal to or greater than the Avalanche of Flesh value shown on this model's damage table.

Regenerating Monstrosity: *Hell Pit Abominations are notoriously difficult to slay, and can even regrow severed limbs.*

In your hero phase, you can heal up to D3 wounds allocated to this model.

Terrifying: *This horrific monstrosity strikes fear deep into the hearts of its enemies.*

Subtract 1 from the Bravery characteristic of enemy units while they are within 3" of any models with this ability.

Warpstone Spikes: *The warpstone spikes driven into the flesh of a Hell Pit Abomination make it highly resistant to magical spells.*

Each time this model is affected by a spell or endless spell, you can roll a dice. If you do so, on a 4+ ignore the effects of that spell on this model.

Too Horrible to Die: *As a Hell Pit Abomination twitches its last shuddering death throes, there is a chance its unholy metabolism will restart one of its many foul hearts, or at the very least that its carcass will disgorge the revolting tide of parasitic rats that had been gnawing upon its innards.*

The first time this model is slain, before removing it from the battlefield, roll a dice and look up the roll on the table below.

D6   Result

1-2   *Dead:* Remove this model from play as normal.

3-4   *The Rats Emerge:* All units within 3" of this model immediately suffer D3 mortal wounds. Then remove this model from play.

5-6   *It's Alive!:* This model is not slain. Instead, you must heal D6 wounds allocated to it, and any wounds or mortal wounds that remain to be allocated to it are negated.

KEYWORDS	CHAOS, SKAVENTIDE, CLANS MOULDER, FIGHTING BEAST, MONSTER, HELL PIT ABOMINATION

RAT OGORS

Monstrous brutes of stitched muscle, melded flesh, lashing talons and snapping jaws, the Rat Ogors of the Clans Moulder are terrifying war beasts whose packs rip through the enemy ranks in a storm of flying limbs and jetting gore.

MISSILE WEAPONS	Range	Attacks	To Hit	To Wound	Rend	Damage
Warpfire Gun	16"	1	5+	3+	-1	D3
MELEE WEAPONS	**Range**	**Attacks**	**To Hit**	**To Wound**	**Rend**	**Damage**
Tearing Claws, Blades and Fangs	1"	4	4+	3+	-1	2

DESCRIPTION

A unit of Rat Ogors has any number of models, each armed with Tearing Claws, Blades and Fangs. 1 in every 2 models can also be armed with a Warpfire Gun.

ABILITIES

Rabid Fury: *The snarling rage of a blood-frenzied Rat Ogor pack is a truly terrifying sight to behold.*

If the unmodified hit roll for an attack made with Tearing Claws, Blades and Fangs is 6, that attack inflicts 2 hits on the target instead of 1. Make a wound and save roll for each hit.

KEYWORDS	CHAOS, SKAVEN, SKAVENTIDE, CLANS MOULDER, FIGHTING BEAST, PACK, RAT OGORS

RAT SWARMS

When the skaven go to war, their clawpacks often advance amidst a teeming tide of vermin. Immense swarms of rats seethe across the field of battle, engulfing those who fall and devouring any unfortunate enough to stand in their path.

MELEE WEAPONS	Range	Attacks	To Hit	To Wound	Rend	Damage
Gnawing Teeth	1"	5	5+	5+	-	1

DESCRIPTION

A unit of Rat Swarms has any number of models, each armed with Gnawing Teeth.

ABILITIES

Endless Tide of Rats: *There are always more rats, and more, and more, and even more.*

In your hero phase you can return 1 slain model to this unit. Set up the returning model within 1" of this unit. The returning model can only be set up within 3" of an enemy unit if this unit is already within 3" of that enemy unit.

KEYWORDS	CHAOS, SKAVENTIDE, CLANS MOULDER, PACK, RAT SWARMS

GIANT RATS

MOVE 8"
WOUNDS 1
SAVE -
BRAVERY 3

Growing up to the size of a Gryph-hound, Giant Rats hunt in huge packs that can overwhelm entire enemy regiments and drag down even the most monstrous foes through sheer weight of numbers.

MELEE WEAPONS	Range	Attacks	To Hit	To Wound	Rend	Damage
Vicious Teeth	1"	1	4+	5+	-	1

DESCRIPTION

A unit of Giant Rats has any number of models, each armed with Vicious Teeth.

ABILITIES

Wave of Rats: *In combat, Giant Rats frantically scramble over each other in their savage eagerness to devour the foe.*

While a unit of Giant Rats has 10 or more models, the Range characteristic of its Vicious Teeth is 2" instead of 1". While a unit of Giant Rats has 20 or more models, the Range characteristic of its Vicious Teeth is 3" instead of 1".

KEYWORDS	CHAOS, SKAVENTIDE, CLANS MOULDER, PACK, GIANT RATS

DEATHMASTER

MOVE 7"
WOUNDS 5
SAVE 4+
BRAVERY 5

Elite assassins and masters of murder, the Deathmasters of the Clans Eshin are so skilled as to seem supernatural in their abilities. Bursting from amidst the mass of skaven in a sudden whirling of blades and fangs, they slay their victims swiftly.

MISSILE WEAPONS	Range	Attacks	To Hit	To Wound	Rend	Damage
Eshin Throwing Stars	12"	4	4+	5+	-	1
MELEE WEAPONS	**Range**	**Attacks**	**To Hit**	**To Wound**	**Rend**	**Damage**
Weeping Blades	1"	3	3+	3+	-1	D3
Fighting Claws	1"	7	3+	3+	-	1

DESCRIPTION

A Deathmaster is a single model armed with one of the following weapon options: Eshin Throwing Stars and Weeping Blades; or Eshin Throwing Stars and Fighting Claws.

ABILITIES

Hidden Killer: *Deathmasters often hide themselves amidst the ranks of skaven regiments.*

Instead of setting up this model on the battlefield, you can place it to one side and say that it is set up in hiding as a reserve unit. If you do so, at the start of a combat phase, you can set up this model within 1" of a friendly **SKAVENTIDE** unit that has 5 or more models and a Wounds characteristic of 1. If this model is not set up on the battlefield before the start of the fourth battle round, it is slain.

Running Death: *Eshin warriors are trained in a unique fighting style that allows them to attack with incredible speed and dexterity.*

This model can run and still shoot later in the same turn.

Throwing Stars: *Eshin throwing stars are hurled at the foe in rapid volleys.*

If the unmodified hit roll for an attack made with Eshin Throwing Stars is 6, that attack inflicts 2 hits on the target instead of 1. Make a wound and save roll for each hit.

KEYWORDS	CHAOS, SKAVEN, SKAVENTIDE, CLANS ESHIN, HERO, DEATHMASTER

124

WOUNDS	MOVE	SAVE
1	7"	5+
	5	
	BRAVERY	

● WARSCROLL ●

GUTTER RUNNERS

Emerging from positions of concealment at the enemy's flanks and rear, Gutter Runners fall upon their victims in a storm of flashing blades, hurtling throwing stars and viciously bared fangs.

MISSILE WEAPONS	Range	Attacks	To Hit	To Wound	Rend	Damage
Eshin Throwing Stars	12"	2	4+	5+	-	1
MELEE WEAPONS	**Range**	**Attacks**	**To Hit**	**To Wound**	**Rend**	**Damage**
Punch Dagger and Blade	1"	2	3+	4+	-1	1

DESCRIPTION

A unit of Gutter Runners has any number of models, each armed with a Punch Dagger and Blade, and Eshin Throwing Stars.

ABILITIES

Running Death: *Eshin warriors are trained in a unique fighting style that allows them to attack with incredible speed and dexterity.*

This unit can run and still shoot later in the same turn.

Sneaky Infiltrators: *Gutter Runners are masters of stealth, and can sneak up on almost anyone.*

Instead of setting up this unit on the battlefield, you can place it to one side and say that it is infiltrating in reserve. If you do so, at the end of your first movement phase, you must set up this unit wholly within 6" of the edge of the battlefield and more than 9" from any enemy units.

Throwing Stars: *Eshin throwing stars are hurled at the foe in rapid volleys.*

If the unmodified hit roll for an attack made with Eshin Throwing Stars is 6, that attack inflicts 2 hits on the target instead of 1. Make a wound and save roll for each hit.

KEYWORDS	CHAOS, SKAVEN, SKAVENTIDE, CLANS ESHIN, GUTTER RUNNERS

WOUNDS	MOVE	SAVE
1	7"	6+
	4	
	BRAVERY	

● WARSCROLL ●

NIGHT RUNNERS

Swift and sneaky, clawpacks of Night Runners envelop their enemies before launching vicious assaults to lay them low with volleys of throwing weapons and well-placed blades between the ribs.

MISSILE WEAPONS	Range	Attacks	To Hit	To Wound	Rend	Damage
Eshin Throwing Weapons	12"	1	4+	5+	-	1
MELEE WEAPONS	**Range**	**Attacks**	**To Hit**	**To Wound**	**Rend**	**Damage**
Stabbing Blade	1"	1	4+	4+	-	1

DESCRIPTION

A unit of Night Runners has any number of models, each armed with a Stabbing Blade and Eshin Throwing Weapons.

NIGHTLEADER: 1 model in this unit can be a Nightleader. Add 1 to the Attacks characteristic of that model's Stabbing Blade.

ABILITIES

Running Death: *Eshin warriors are trained in a unique fighting style that allows them to attack with incredible speed and dexterity.*

This unit can run and still shoot later in the same turn.

Slinking Advance: *Night Runners scurry ahead of the main body of a skaven army to harass and slow down the foe.*

After armies are set up, but before the first battle round begins, you can move this unit up to 2D6".

Throwing Weapons: *Eshin throwing weapons are hurled at the foe in rapid volleys.*

If the unmodified hit roll for an attack made with Eshin Throwing Weapons is 6, that attack inflicts 2 hits on the target instead of 1. Make a wound and save roll for each hit.

KEYWORDS	CHAOS, SKAVEN, SKAVENTIDE, CLANS ESHIN, NIGHT RUNNERS

VERMINTIDE

An endless tide of unholy vermin pours through the cracks in reality, their eyes aglow and their fangs unnaturally sharp. This conjured swarm can strip even an armoured warrior to the bone in moments.

DESCRIPTION

Vermintide is a single model.

PREDATORY: Vermintide is a predatory endless spell. It can move up to 7".

MAGIC

Summon Vermintide: *A skaven spellcaster can summon forth a seething mass of arcane rodents and vermin that consumes everything in its path.*

Summon Vermintide has a casting value of 7. Only **SKAVENTIDE WIZARDS** can attempt to cast this spell. If successfully cast, set up a Vermintide model wholly within 13" of the caster.

ABILITIES

Ravening Horde: *A Vermintide rips and tears indiscriminately at anything in its path.*

After this model has moved, the player that moved it can pick 1 unit within 3" of this model and roll 13 dice. For each 6, that unit suffers 1 mortal wound.

In addition, roll 13 dice for each unit that finishes a normal move or a charge move within 3" of this model. For each 6, that unit suffers 1 mortal wound.

Voracious Hunger: *The unnatural creatures of a Vermintide possess a terrible hunger that only the consumption of raw flesh can sate.*

When this model is set up, the player who set it up can immediately make a move with it.

Ratkin: *A Vermintide will not harm other rodent-beasts, and will allow them to pass by unhindered.*

SKAVENTIDE units are not affected by the Ravening Horde ability. In addition, **SKAVENTIDE** models can move across this model in the same manner as a model that can fly.

KEYWORDS	ENDLESS SPELL, VERMINTIDE

WARP LIGHTNING VORTEX

A hurled clawful of warpstone shards swell rapidly in size until they become hovering prisms that crackle furiously with warp lightning. Green-black bolts flash back and forth, forming a lethal cage of energy that blasts apart any who approach too closely.

DESCRIPTION

Warp Lightning Vortex is a single endless spell that consists of 3 models (if it is dispelled, remove all 3 models).

MAGIC

Summon Warp Lightning Vortex: *Warpstone shards are cast into the air, growing impossibly large and discharging bolts of warp lightning.*

Summon Warp Lightning Vortex has a casting value of 8. Only **SKAVENTIDE WIZARDS** can attempt to cast this spell. If successfully cast, set up 1 Warp Lightning Vortex model wholly within 26" of the caster, then set up the second and third Warp Lightning Vortex models exactly 7" from the first model and exactly 7" from each other (the models will form a triangle with each model exactly 7" from the other two models).

ABILITIES

Warp Lightning Bolts: *Coruscating bolts of warp lightning leap outwards from the Warp Lightning Vortex, obliterating those nearby.*

When this model is set up, and at the end of each movement phase, roll 1 dice for each unit within 6" of any of the models from this endless spell. Add 1 to the dice roll if that unit is within 6" of two of the models from this endless spell. Add 2 to the dice roll instead of 1 if that unit is within 6" of all three models from this endless spell. On a 4+ that unit suffers D3 mortal wounds. On an unmodified roll of 6, that unit suffers D6 mortal wounds instead of D3 mortal wounds.

Warp Vortex: *The sheer destructive anarchy that surrounds a Warp Lightning Vortex slows the progress of warriors caught in its midst.*

Units cannot run or fly when they make a normal move that starts within 6" of any models from this endless spell.

KEYWORDS	ENDLESS SPELL, WARP LIGHTNING VORTEX

BELL OF DOOM

Swirling vapours boil from the yawning maw of the spell's caster, billowing into an unnatural cloud. Lightning flashes amidst the gloomy mass, silhouetting a huge bell that swings in mid-air, tolling out the doom of those who dare resist the skaventide.

DESCRIPTION

Bell of Doom is a single model.

PREDATORY: Bell of Doom is a predatory endless spell. It can move up to 13" and can fly.

MAGIC

Summon Bell of Doom: *Invoking ancient creation myths, the spellcaster causes a great Bell of Doom to manifest upon the battlefield.*

Summon Bell of Doom has a casting value of 6. Only **Skaventide Wizards** can attempt to cast this spell. If successfully cast, set up a Bell of Doom model wholly within 13" of the caster.

ABILITIES

Apocalyptic Doom: *With a deafening explosion, the Bell of Doom splits asunder.*

Roll 3D6 after this model is set up or finishes a move. On a roll of 13, each unit within 13" of this model suffers D3 mortal wounds. This model is then dispelled.

Boldness or Despair: *The dreadful ringing of the Bell of Doom fills the minds of the skaven's foes with a deep despair, while emboldening the normally cowardly ratmen.*

Do not take battleshock tests for **Skaventide** units while they are within 13" of this model. Subtract 1 from the Bravery characteristic of any other units while they are within 13" of this model.

KEYWORDS	ENDLESS SPELL, BELL OF DOOM

The air crackles with the leaping arcs of the Warp Lightning Vortex, the ground seethes with the scurry and squirm of the Vermintide, and over it all rolls the ceaseless, malevolent tolling of the Bell of Doom as the endless spells of the skaven are unleashed.

PITCHED BATTLE PROFILES

The table below provides points, minimum and maximum unit sizes, and battlefield roles for the warscrolls and warscroll battalions in this book, for use in Pitched Battles. Spending the points listed on this table allows you to take a minimum-sized unit with any of its upgrades. Understrength units cost the full amount of points. Larger units are taken in multiples of their minimum unit size; multiply their cost by the same amount as you multiplied their size. If a unit has two points values separated by a slash (e.g. '60/200'), the second value is for a maximum sized unit. Units that are listed as 'Unique' are named characters and can only be taken once in an army. A unit that has any of the keywords listed on the Allies table can be taken as an allied unit by a Skaventide army. Updated February 2019; the profiles printed here take precedence over any profiles with an earlier publication date or no publication date.

SKAVENTIDE UNIT	UNIT SIZE MIN	UNIT SIZE MAX	POINTS	BATTLEFIELD ROLE	NOTES
Plagueclaw	1	1	160	Artillery	
Warp Lightning Cannon	1	1	180	Artillery	
Warplock Jezzails	3	12	140	Artillery	
Clanrats	20	40	120/200	Battleline	
Doomwheel	1	1	160	Behemoth	
Hell Pit Abomination	1	1	220	Behemoth	
Arch-Warlock	1	1	160	Leader	
Clawlord	1	1	100	Leader	
Deathmaster	1	1	100	Leader	
Grey Seer	1	1	120	Leader	
Master Moulder	1	1	100	Leader	
Plague Priest	1	1	80	Leader	
Skritch Spiteclaw	1	1		Leader	Unique. These units must be taken as a set for a total of 140 points. Although taken as a set, each is a separate unit.
Spiteclaw's Swarm	4	4	140		
Warlock Bombardier	1	1	100	Leader	
Warlock Engineer	1	1	100	Leader	
Grey Seer on Screaming Bell	1	1	200	Leader, Behemoth	
Lord Skreech Verminking	1	1	300	Leader, Behemoth	Unique
Plague Priest on Plague Furnace	1	1	180	Leader, Behemoth	
Thanquol on Boneripper	1	1	400	Leader, Behemoth	Unique
Verminlord Corruptor	1	1	260	Leader, Behemoth	
Verminlord Deceiver	1	1	300	Leader, Behemoth	
Verminlord Warbringer	1	1	260	Leader, Behemoth	
Verminlord Warpseer	1	1	260	Leader, Behemoth	
Doom-Flayer	1	1	60		
Giant Rats	10	40	60/200		Battleline in Skaventide army if general is MASTERCLAN or CLANS MOULDER, and all other units are CLANS MOULDER
Gutter Runners	5	20	60/200		Battleline in Skaventide army if general is MASTERCLAN or CLANS ESHIN, and all other units are CLANS ESHIN

SKAVENTIDE UNIT	UNIT SIZE MIN	MAX	POINTS	BATTLEFIELD ROLE	NOTES
Night Runners	10	40	80/280		Battleline in Skaventide army if general is **MASTERCLAN** or **CLANS ESHIN**, and all other units are **CLANS ESHIN**
Packmasters	3	12	60		
Plague Censer Bearers	5	20	60		Battleline in Skaventide army if general is **MASTERCLAN** or **CLANS PESTILENS**, and all other units are **CLANS PESTILENS**
Plague Monks	10	40	70/240		Battleline in Skaventide army if general is **MASTERCLAN** or **CLANS PESTILENS**, and all other units are **CLANS PESTILENS**
Rat Ogors	2	8	100		Battleline in Skaventide army if general is **MASTERCLAN** or **CLANS MOULDER**, and all other units are **CLANS MOULDER**
Rat Swarms	2	8	60		
Ratling Gun	1	1	80		
Skryre Acolytes	5	30	60/320		Battleline in Skaventide army if general is **MASTERCLAN** or **CLANS SKRYRE**, and all other units are **CLANS SKRYRE**
Stormfiends	3	9	260		Battleline in Skaventide army if general is **MASTERCLAN** or **CLANS SKRYRE**, and all other units are **CLANS SKRYRE**
Stormvermin	10	40	140/500		Battleline in Skaventide army
Warpfire Thrower	1	1	70		
Warp-Grinder	1	1	80		
Congregation of Filth	-	-	160	*Warscroll Battalion*	
Fleshmeld Menagerie	-	-	160	*Warscroll Battalion*	
Foulrain Congregation	-	-	110	*Warscroll Battalion*	
Claw-horde	-	-	180	*Warscroll Battalion*	
Plaguesmog Congregation	-	-	120	*Warscroll Battalion*	
Slinktalon	-	-	160	*Warscroll Battalion*	
Virulent Procession	-	-	100	*Warscroll Battalion*	
Warpcog Convocation	-	-	60	*Warscroll Battalion*	
Arkhspark Voltik	-	-	110	*Enginecoven*	
Gascloud Chokelung	-	-	120	*Enginecoven*	
Gautfyre Skorch	-	-	140	*Enginecoven*	Can only be taken as part of a Warpcog Convocation
Rattlegauge Warplock	-	-	120	*Enginecoven*	
Whyrlblade Threshik	-	-	130	*Enginecoven*	
Bell of Doom	*1*	*1*	*40*	*Endless Spell*	
Vermintide	*1*	*1*	*40*	*Endless Spell*	
Warp Lightning Vortex	*1*	*1*	*100*	*Endless Spell*	
Gnawhole	*1*	*1*	*0*	*Scenery*	

CHAOS	ALLIES
Skaventide	Nurgle (only if general is **CLANS PESTILENS**)